RELEASED
from the
WATCHTOWER

D0544397

RELEASED
from the
WATCHTOWER

VALERIE TOMSETT

Foreword by Canon J. Stafford Wright

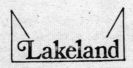

LAKELAND
BLUNDELL HOUSE
GOODWOOD ROAD
LONDON S.E.14

ISBN 0 551 00049 X

Printed in Great Britain by
Willmer Brothers Limited, Birkenhead
and bound by Tinlings of Liverpool

Foreword

I do not know Valerie Tomsett, but, when I started to read the typescript of this book, I had to read it through to the end at one sitting. There are several excellent books on the teachings of Jehovah's Witnesses, and those that are written by ex-Witnesses are especially helpful, since only one who has been a member can convey the feelings and experiences of the Movement.

Yet, so far as I know, there is no book by an ordinary woman, who first as daughter and later as wife, was caught up by the Witnesses. Those of us who speak on the subject are usually fairly formal in our discussion of their false doctrines Here is someone who recreates the appalling family life of Jehovah's Witnesses, and who shows how this arises from the ideas that they are taught. She writes for the heart as well as for the head. What a picture the book would make if it could be written up as a film!

We see the utter lack of natural feeling and sympathy in the Witnesses. The author writes of her family after they had become members: "We had been a happy family once, but suddenly we weren't any more." Of her mother: "I might meet one of two people—a mother or a Jehovah's Witness."

In her door-to-door work Mrs. Tomsett was at times rebuked by fellow Witnesses because she preferred to talk with other Christians of beliefs that they had in common instead of pounding them with propaganda. When at last she attended a Christian Bible study, she found amazing relief in being able to search the Scriptures freely together to discover their teaching instead of being drilled in what she had to believe.

I hope this book will have a wide circulation. It could be an eye-opener to people who are impressed with the apparent zeal and sincerity of the Witnesses; and it will give more than a peep behind the scenes to those who rightly are concerned with meeting false doctrine with true. It could profitably be lent to Witnesses themselves, particularly at an early stage in their indoctrination, or when they begin to feel some honest doubts about the Movement, yet do not know what to do for fear that their doubts are from the devil.

J. STAFFORD WRIGHT

Contents

Introduction

Before I begin this story I would like to make it clear that I do not write with any bitterness against certain people whom I shall mention, for my belief is that they themselves hardly realize what they are doing. But, after so many experiences at their hands, it would be wrong for me to be silent, or else people may suffer ruin because they do not turn to God for protection.

I realize that I have kept quiet far too long, and while I have been silent many have taken up with false beliefs, and the true Christian faith has suffered.

What I set down here is true; it all happened to my family and to me—a very ordinary suburban family—but thousands of people all over the world could tell the same story, and there is a warning here to all who value life and family, not to accept doctrines other than those of the true Church which preaches Christ. Utter disintegration of life in all aspects of living will be the result else, without help from anywhere; least of all from the members of these sects; least of all from the anonymous leaders of the Witnesses and the authors of their publications.

I would like to thank all the followers of Christ who welcomed me back into belief in Him as my personal Saviour, for their prayer support, and above all their Christian love and encouragement. These things I have greatly appreciated.

As time goes by my faith in Christ is being firmly established upon promises made through the Holy Scriptures: "When my father and my mother forsake me, then the LORD will take me up." (Psalm 27:10.) and within the context of this Spiritual adoption the words found in Hebrews 13:5, "I will never leave thee, nor forsake thee." is a binding covenant.

My Watchtower adversaries may well ridicule my faith as being negative in knowledge, and endeavour to persuade my readers that I am devil-possessed or mentally deranged, however, my assurance is in Christ as a living answer to heresies and the influence behind: "If God be for us (me), who can be against us (me)?" (Romans 8:31).

V.T.

I

Happiness

And they went down both into the water, both Philip and the eunuch; and he baptized him . . . and he went on his way rejoicing. (Acts 8: 38, 39).

Sunday, 14th May 1967 was a very important date in my life, for that day I stepped into the baptistry of a church in Hove. All I wanted to do was to weep, weep for the utter joy of coming face to face with Christ, and simply saying, "I believe!"

Believe what?

I believe that Jesus, Son of God, lived here on earth two thousand years ago; that He was born of the Virgin Mary; that He glorified the Father in His baptism, His ministry and in the healing of the sick; that He was crucified, that He died and was buried, that He rose again on the third day and appeared to His disciples, and was with them constantly until He ascended into heaven. Then, as I believe, the Holy Spirit descended upon the believers in Christ—the Comforter whom He had promised before His death.

I believe that the power and glory of Christ is the same yesterday, today and for ever.

I believe that the scriptures are the fruit of the Holy Spirit—given by inspiration of God, and not mere literary work of man.

I believe that from my early days the Lord's hand was upon me, and that He has given me the wonderful privilege of making a long and difficult pilgrimage. For a time I completely lost contact with Him, and then quite unexpectedly He grasped me kindly and firmly by both hands and said, "Your battle is over; follow Me. I am the way and truth and the life. Whosoever believeth in Me shall not perish, but have everlasting life."

As I entered the water that day, I felt that the long

9

years of life had reached a climax, and that my spiritual future was safe with our Lord, as my light and guide until the day of His coming. The text which was given to me, seconds before my immersion, was:

"I am the light of the world; he that followeth me shall not walk in darkness, but shall have the light of life" John 8:12 and no verse could have been more appropriate.

With the armour of the Holy Spirit as my protection against the devil's wiles, my days to come would be filled with the Lord's blessing and love, like the foretaste which He had given me during the few previous months since my conversion.

My baptism was for me, as Peter puts it "an appeal to God for a clear conscience, through the resurrection of Jesus Christ" (1 Peter 3:21 RSV).

Already I was overwhelmed by the love and the blessings our Lord was showering upon me, the privilege of washing away my past sins in the baptism of repentance. Since then He has enveloped me in such a power and warmth, which has changed everything, and my full experiences have been too wonderful to explain fully. I certainly was "changed in the twinkling of an eye from being dead in sin, to live unto righteousness in Christ". I am the least of all humankind to deserve His forgiveness, for I had been one who paid no heed nor thought to a deeper, more spiritual life—one who was wrapped up in the things of this life. Jesus said "I am not come to call the righteous, but sinners to repentance" (Matt. 9:13), and He is long-suffering to us-ward, not willing that any should perish, but that all should come to repentance. Praise the Lord!

Prayers and intercessions which had been offered ten or sixteen years before were at last being answered. The wonder of it all!

Already John 8: 31-32 is becoming real for me; "If you continue in my word, ye are my disciples indeed; and you shall know the truth, and the truth shall make you free". I *am* free to worship our Lord; free from the slavery of worldly pleasures, and not a slave to fear and the dark depression which comes from the devil's deception and from selfish desires.

2

First Sight

As new born babes, desire the sincere milk of the word, that ye may grow thereby. (I Peter 2:2).

As a child I attended Sunday schools at one or other of the local Free Churches. The death of Christ on the Cross made a great impression upon me, and the agony and suffering He went through always meant very much to me.

I remember at that time the packed churches, as people besought God that we might have victory over the oncoming invasion of Hitler's armies. They seemed to realize that only God's power could help us to withstand such a mighty show of force by the enemy, and in addition to the attacks by land, sea and air, there now came the guided missiles, unmanned aircraft, which increased the enemy's threat enormously.

At last the nation's prayers were answered, and peace came to our shores. The promise of 2 Chron. 20:27 had come true: "the Lord had made them to rejoice over their enemies."

As a child I suffered greatly from asthma, and this affected my education; so much so that the doctor recommended a boarding-school, and a place was found for me in Kent. In great fear and trembling I set off early, one bright September morning, ready to begin the new school year. I had read so many books about the times they had at boarding school that my imagination ran riot!—visits to the tuckshop (I was sure that sweets and cakes from there must taste far better than anything I had ever eaten!). Then there were midnight bun-fights, raids on the pantry, apple-pie beds, and climbing over the wall for visits to the local cinema, which was out of bounds; so that I was looking forward to being educated away from home. However, my excitement waned, and by the time the day of my departure dawned I was filled with great apprehension, and my vision of a beautiful school with huge windows, letting in the glorious sunshine, with lovely grounds and a swimming pool, all faded fast, and I dreaded instead the prospect of a dark, dismal, work-house-like building, befitting the tales of Dickens. There would be female monsters, not attractive and vivacious mistresses. How I wished that the ground would swallow me up, or (even better) that the train might turn round and take me home!

We changed trains at Hastings and again at Ashford, and soon another train took me to my destination.

My emotion of fear was soon to be replaced by that of surprise, for I found myself in a Roman Catholic Convent. No one had thought of the religious side of my education, though it had been taken for granted that I would be sent to some Protestant place. The sisters were kind, and the school was beautiful, with its own grounds and a private beach; but all this was lost on me. I wanted to go home; I missed my parents, my friends and all the familiar surroundings of my home town. I must have been a trial to these nuns, with my tear-stained face and my refusal to eat food which I felt would choke me. The time dragged by; the first week, the second, the third, and at last the fourth—the fourth Sunday, our monthly visiting day! I was glad to see my parents, but over the day there hung the grim fact that it would soon be over, and I would have to wait another whole month before I saw them again.

But as time slipped by I began to be absorbed in the convent life, and I loved the school and the lessons. These nuns seemed to have something that my day-school had lacked—the ability to bring out the best in us. Though I did not realize it then, this paved the way for better things later on. Even today I can only thank the Lord for the privilege of witnessing so early their profound devotions, and seeing the importance of prayer. There was grace, and prayer before we started school, and for protection before we started out on walks. Everything in the course of the day was commended in prayer. One of the loveliest times of prayer was at six in the evening, when a bell would be rung, so wherever we were we might be called to prayer. Immediately, we bowed our heads and were quiet for a few minutes, and this taught us not only the way of prayer but obedience—for whatever we are doing, Jesus comes first.

Often Sundays were set aside as complete days of prayer, and we were encouraged to use the Chapel for private devotion. Even as children we benefited from this. This was convent life, neither hurried nor marred by the hustle and bustle of the twentieth century. Many people say that the retreat into the cloisters is escapism, but in fact a nun faces a hard and gruelling life in giving up all worldly possessions, and in taking up the cross and answering her calling, whether this be in a "closed" order, where their lives are devoted to prayer and supplication, or a "working" order, which might serve in anything from teaching, to nursing in a leper colony. This particular order of nuns specialized in teaching, both here and abroad.

The school impressed upon me for ever the importance of prayer. Protestants there joined only in the service of Benediction; the remainder of our devotional time was spent in private prayer, particularly after the Sisters' Mass on Sunday mornings, when we met for prayer in the little chapel, fragrant with incense, and eloquent of the humility and majesty, the beauty and dignity of prayer.

Yet even in this holy place we faced the same temptations as in the world; it was not easy to attend chapel in the right attitude of mind. On one occasion I remember grumbling a good deal about the length of the service, and about kneeling for so long. I declared that I would never walk straight again, and that my knees must be set permanently in a kneeling position! One of the Sisters very gently reminded me that our Lord didn't grumble when He died for me!

Once, during a very persistent attack of asthma, a Sister sat me by the window in the dormitory, but nothing would shift it; and then I was taught to tell the Lord about it, not demanding relief, but indicating that for His sake I would carry my cross (Matt. 10:38, 16:

24), but always keeping in mind the power of God to over-rule.

When the doctor came for our three-monthly medical check-up, the asthma had eased considerably; I had gone a whole month without an attack. It seemed likely that I might be able to live at home and attend day-school without frequent absences, but that would not be for another month. How those four weeks dragged by! Would the day never come for my release? Back into the world—to be free! To escape at last! I forgot the things that had made me happy in the convent, and longed only to get away. So those poor nuns had another month of childish tantrums—not tears this time, but downright wilful revolutionary disobedience. When the day of my departure arrived, I am sure that it was with great relief that they shut and bolted the door behind me!

As a Protestant I had entered the Roman Catholic convent, and as a Protestant I left; we had lived together, each respecting the other's belief without treading on each other's spiritual toes.

3

Outer Darkness

Weeping may endure for a night. (Psalm 30:5).

On my return home there was the problem of starting
a new school year. I needed to enter as a senior pupil
and very much wanted to be educated at a Roman
Catholic convent as a day scholar, but had to resign
myself to a state school. As the winter approached,
and I was subject to the harsh elements of the rain,
wind and cold, my asthma returned in full force, and
in the years that followed I was worse than I had been
before those months away in Kent. The next three
years were spent mostly in bed, with rare visits to
school.

In desperation my Mother sought the aid of a healer
whom she had read about in one of the Sunday papers,
who was believed to have cured many people. My
parents rather suspected that he was a spiritualist and
were very hesitant in taking me to him for treatment,
but after much debate they decided that it might be
the right way. This was the beginning of three to four
years spent in following spiritualism—that "religion"
with a satanic force behind it which takes the
bereaved, the sick and the lame as its prey, deceiving
people with the promise of experiences from the unknown.

Long before I was born my Mother had been taken to
a seance by a kindly landlady. She was told that there
was a young girl there with her, about seven years of
age, dressed in a white robe and wearing a wreath of
roses on her head. My mother's sister had died from
diphtheria at that age, but what was this about a wreath
of roses? When my Mother next saw my grandmother
she told her this story, but added that she thought that
the "wreath" was a bit silly! The colour drained away

from my grandmother's face, for this opened old wounds, and she told my Mother that her sister had suffered so much and so bravely during the period in hospital that when she died the nurses who had cared for her went into the hospital grounds to pick roses, to make a wreath for her head. Only my grandparents knew of that very lovely, and to them sacred, gesture. My grandmother had made my Mother promise faithfully never to attend such a meeting again.

Now after all these years the temptation to break that promise was powerful, though it seemed more important to uphold the promise, for grandmother had since died. This would also mean disobedience to God's word, for the scriptures warn us against spiritualism.

Only God knows the conflict which went on in my parents' minds when they read the newspaper article; I was desperately ill at that time, as, in addition to the asthma (which was leading to comas) my temperature would rise to 105° without apparent reason. So I was taken for treatment; but it proved a waste of time and money.

But although our misgivings continued, this initial disappointment only gave us an appetite to search into spiritualism, to find a genuine healer, and to receive messages from our departed relatives. Although I had not been healed, Mother still believed in spiritual healing. She was suddenly taken ill, and the doctor said that she must have an operation immediately. She said that she could not leave me, because my attacks were far too frequent and severe, and asked for time before deciding. This gave her the chance to call on the aid of a healer, who confirmed that she needed an operation—a spiritual one. She was to be in bed by ten o'clock, and to lie very quiet and still. I cannot recall exactly what happened on the promised evening of the "spiritual operation", but I do remember her speaking of strange sensations in her body; nothing painful, but probing and continuous. The following morning she was completely healed. Something very remarkable had occurred; a complaint, very painful and obvious one day, had wholly disappeared by the next.

Now we had our appetite really whetted! though it

was one thing to seek healing, but another to call up the dead, and I remember her misgivings over this. My parents discussed the matter long and anxiously before they joined in the seances. Indeed, the first message that my Mother did receive, spoke of this spiritual wrestling within her (she had in fact walked round the streets before entering the building) and she was assured that her own mother was close by, and had, in fact, given her the final push into the meeting! She fell for this hook line and sinker, and, as we were to realize in the years that followed, there was some shrewd psychology behind it all.

I must bear witness that we met there just a few healers who acknowledged that their gift was from the Lord. They put themselves at the disposal of the sick at any time of day or night. These showed sincerity, compassion for the sick, and an honest belief that their gift was from the Lord, and they used it in scriptural ways. As for money, they left it to patients to give what they could afford. But this was far from being the attitude of other healers, whose aim was to get every penny they could out of the sickness and trials of others.

During that time I had treatment from several mediums and healers, and from some who called themselves chiropractors and osteopaths. My parents spent a small fortune on these deceivers, but my asthma was still there, despite the promises of a cure from treatment which cost a guinea a visit—three visits a week. Seances would provide yet another "supernatural message" which sent us on to yet another healer, but only to face another disappointment. How often we looked forward to a glorious day when I might receive the long-awaited cure, and might breathe like anyone else, and shout with joy, "*I am cured!*" But it never happened.

Despite this, I must confess that Spiritualism fascinated us, and—since twenty or thirty years ago medical science seemed to have little or no help to give, spiritualism and the supernatural seemed to give the only hope of a cure. My first healer had been recommended by a friend of the family; he was known as a "chiropractor": spiritualism was not mentioned, but after my treatment we spent long hours listening to his experiences of the other world. One of his specialities was to predict one's life-span—he himself would live to ninety-two, whilst mine was a mere fourteen years. However, other clairvoyants assured my Mother that although I was very ill, she need not be anxious, for I was an example of the creaking gate lasting the longest. There was obviously no liaison in the spirit-world on this matter! and this sowed one seed of doubt—to be confirmed about four years later, when we were told at a meeting that he had passed over, about twenty years short of his reckoning! The medium and her husband were carrying on his work, and I could with confidence be placed in their care. Mother was thrilled about this, and lost no time in making an appointment for me. Young as I was, I sensed something spurious about this, and my intuition was to be proved right. Their home was on the sea front at Lancing, and I was interested to see upon their walls several drawings of their spirit-guides—none of whom had died in the faith of Christ, but were Red Indians or Chinese. They told me that I had two guides —a French dancer and a nun. This was supposed to account for my conflicting personality—one minute full of life and active, and the next quiet and studious, with a special love for nuns. They drew me a picture of "my" nun; it was most disappointing; rather doll-like, with watery blue eyes. She seemed to lack the character and stability of the nuns I had known.

The house seemed to be filled with poltergeists, for cushions and various objects were flung about the rooms during the meetings, and there was a sense of general disorder. Was it just trickery on a human level, or was the house filled with some satanic force? I only know that even before I met these people I sensed something counterfeit about them, and this remained with me throughout the time I knew them.

They were absolute rogues, and gave me all sorts of stuff under the name of "herb medicine". They also suggested a glass of milk daily, with beaten raw egg and sugar added. This, of course, has high protein value and formed a good basic nourishing diet for me. Heavy meals do aggravate chest complaints. But that wasn't their reason for offering this "daily pinta"; according to them the raw egg-white would form a skin on my lungs! So much for these healers' knowledge of the human body. I remember, even now with embarrassment, a ridiculous practice which had to be performed every morning. Mother dug a hole in the garden, and I had to get on all fours and breathe in soil-fumes and exhale to the side. What a ritual! I performed this under protest, and devoutly hoped and prayed that neighbours would be far too busy in the mornings to look out of their windows and see the strange object huddled over a cavity in the garden! When it rained, I still inhaled and exhaled as usual, carefully covered with waterproofs. How relieved I was when illness prevented this procedure!

Even today, with the advance of medical science, thousands of people are still being misled by false "healers", because ordinary people wonder if these methods might work. The real scandal of all this is the financial side—it was a guinea a visit in those days, taken two or three times a week from sick and aged people who could ill afford this, but who were ready to pay out their last penny to get relief from pain.

There is the same abuse with seances. The mediums also are avid for money, and dupe people who have been bereaved of their loved ones. Often the "messages" are nothing but psychological guesswork. It's easy when you know how! Those who attend regularly and are well-known in the fellowship are easy prey, for all sorts of details can be given to the medium before the meeting. It must be added that some messages may come from the other side, for the satanic force is surely very real. Spiritualists always say that one must learn to discriminate between spiritualism and spiritism—the latter being the false and evil power. But this is often difficult until it is too late.

Money! money! money! That was the aim of this "ism"; money for healing, money for a message. Actually, since tips about race-horses and football pools, lucky numbers and colours were all thrown in for the same fee there was always the chance that we might in these ways get back the money we spent; but often that would only result in throwing good money after bad.

We began to wake up to these things, and asked, "Did Christ sell His gifts? Did He bring wagers into the early church?" This, and every kindred question we asked ourselves, could only be answered "No!"

I must add that one of the last "messages" we received in a seance was "Look out for a Rose Grove, or Grover; she will be a great help to you spiritually". At this time we were receiving visits by a woman* who had been calling for as long as I could remember, in order to interest us in her beliefs; when she knew that we were interested in spiritualism she brought us many scriptural proofs that this was the work of the devil. Here was another seed which later bore its fruit.

*See p. 27

4

Sunshine

Joy cometh in the morning. (Psalm 30:5).

The following interlude in my story was extremely brief, but a very happy one. One of my school-friends invited me to her church to join the Christian Endeavour; I went without much enthusiasm but I enjoyed the meeting, and promised to go again. I was surprised to find that Mother objected to this. She had attended that particular church years before, but had left it with very bad feelings, and she used her experiences there as a regular argument against the Church and its clergy. However, the very real Christian fellowship which I had had, both at school and at the little mission, swung the pendulum in their favour rather than home, and once I had made my stand, the door of home was wide open for my new-found church friends and helpers. My mother gave the Endeavourers a wonderful party on my birthday. What a pity that she did not respond to the same offer of fellowship! It would have saved much trouble later on.

All this made me realize how wisely Christ's love deals with us. Certainly He realizes the dangers of loneliness; He Himself was tempted in the solitary wilderness, and the devil attacks us in the same way. Almost every evil action is carried out in isolation; murder, suicide, burglary, sex outrages and the like. Isaiah 29:15 reads "Woe unto them that seek deep to hide their counsel from the Lord, and their works are in the dark, and they say, Who seeth us? And who knoweth us?" He understands our need, for in Hebrews 2:18 we read, "For in that he himself hath suffered being tempted, he is able to succour them that are tempted."

In my present joy and happiness I felt that my

concern for missionary work had been rekindled, and that my ambition might be realized now that I belonged to a church which believed in the Scriptures and in Christ's commandments, especially Matt. 28:19-20, "Go ye therefore, and teach all nations, baptizing them in the name of the Father, and of the Son, and of the Holy Ghost; teaching them to observe all things whatsoever I have commanded you: and, lo, I am with you alway, even unto the end of the world".

When I made my decision for the Lord there were many prayers and great rejoicing. I felt I had come to a climax and that I would most certainly become a missionary.

*   *   *

But at this point there began the new and strange way of life which is the main subject of this book. Was it perhaps the Lord's will that I should leave His fold, wander in so many ways, and finally return to Him? Often, in the days which followed, there was a controlling hand upon me, which saved me from disaster.

5

Autumn

*They know not, neither will they understand;
they walk on in darkness: all the foundations of
the earth are out of course. (Psalm 82:5).*

I was now feeling on top of the world! I was between
fourteen and fifteen—past the time when, according
to expectations and fears, the angel of death should
have been hovering overhead! My health was much
better; I felt wonderful, happy and carefree; my school
work had improved tremendously since I had been
able to attend regularly. It seemed to be just overnight
that I was put into a higher class, and came sixth there.
It was wonderful, too, to enjoy the company of my
friends both at school and at the Mission: I was completely happy!

I went regularly to church on Sunday mornings, Bible
Study in the afternoon and to Christian Endeavour
two evenings a week. I was looking forward to becoming a Sunday School teacher as soon as I was old
enough, and whenever I saw the teachers leading a
class I thought, "That will be *me* one day soon—I hope
I'll succeed!" Yet all the time I had a premonition that
it would not happen . . .

My mother had recently become more and more
friendly with the woman from the Jehovah Witnesses,
who had helped us in our decision to leave spiritualism
alone. When they opened their new Kingdom Hall in
Portslade, my parents accepted an invitation to the
opening service. For eleven years or more they had
failed to respond and now at long last she was beginning
to see the fruits of her labours.

When they got back, they were so excited. What a
wonderful meeting! and *everyone* reading their Bibles!
It was marvellous.

23

The following Sunday I went to morning service at the Mission, and to Bible School in the afternoon; but little did I know then that the day's attendance would be my last, and that I was about to throw in my lot with a sect that preaches and teaches a hatred of the Church which it is difficult to conceive, this side of the Iron Curtain. The new Kingdom Hall was in the same street as the little church which I had been attending and loved so much. There were a lot of people talking in the small forecourt of my own church when I drew near; I walked on the other side of the road, feeling like a traitor. I shuffled past with embarrassment, looking in every direction except my former sanctuary. I felt so guilty! but I was naturally under the guidance of my parents, whom one trusts so implicitly.

The change in my personal life was more noticeable to begin with than the change in my beliefs. My school friends seemed to drift away for no apparent reason— I made a point of not discussing my new beliefs. It seemed impossible to make new friends, for now there seemed to be an invisible barrier between others and myself. I felt very lonely and insecure.

The first requirement at the Kingdom Hall was belief in the battle of Armageddon and the Thousand Glorious Years with Christ on earth—a perfect earth, with no tears, pain, illness or death, just perfection in a wonderful world, with Christ as King and supreme ruler. The vision was marvellous, a dream come true—no more nightmares of war, human bondage, disease—surely this must also mean a *complete* cure for asthma?

The initial intoxication soon wore off when I realized the price of this new world—absolute slavery to the Jehovah's Witness Organization; and this involved complete separation from the world—friends, relatives, education, Queen, Government, Welfare State; everyone and everything not connected with the Society was part of the devil's world and were controlled by him. They bring the words of Scripture to their support— Jesus' prayer in John 17:16, 17, "They are not of the world, even as I am not of the world. Sanctify them through thy truth: thy word is truth"—and also John 15: 18-19, "If the world hate you, ye know that it

24

hated me before it hated you. If ye were of the world, the world would love his own: but because ye are not of the world, but I have chosen you out of the world, therefore the world hateth you."

They point out, too, that Scripture says that Satan himself is transformed into an angel of light (2 Cor. 11:14). It is not surprising, therefore, if his "ministers" appear as "ministers of righteousness' (v. 15), and these are the clergy and ministers of the churches, "whose end shall be according to their works". All Church movements are Satan's schemes to blind the people, and so are international bodies like the United Nations Organization.

Finally, 1 Peter 5:9 also becomes for them a warning to keep apart from the world: "Be sober, be vigilant; because your adversary the devil, as a roaring lion, walketh about, seeking whom he may devour: Whom resist steadfast in the faith, knowing that the same afflictions are accomplished in your brethren that are in the world."

The leaders of the churches are very much the target for the Watchtower firing squad, and in the first of their publications which came into my hands, *Let God Be True*, the first fourteen pages were devoted to attacks upon them. They often used Psalm 116 in these attacks, "I said in my haste, 'All men are liars'", but it is interesting to note that they stop short of verse 13, where the Psalmist says "I will take the cup of salvation and call upon the name of the Lord". Nowhere in its teachings does the Watchtower Society mention that one must receive Christ as a personal Saviour (see Mark 9:37).

Another passage used to attack the clergy is Luke 20:46, 47, "Beware of the scribes, which desire to walk in long robes and love greetings in the markets, and the highest seats in the synagogues, and the chief rooms at feasts; Which devour widows' houses, and for a show make long prayers; the same shall receive greater damnation". So also Matt. 7:15, "Beware of false prophets, which come to you in sheep's clothing, but inwardly they are ravening wolves". The "sheep's clothing" is taken to mean the clerical collar and other ministerial garments. Scripture after scripture is adduced to support slanderous accusations against everyone who does not conform to their school of thought, and very few of my age (for I had not yet left school) could withstand this deft sleight of hand of quotations, apart from the help of the Holy Spirit; but He was unknown to me at that time. From the human standpoint, one would need a university degree in ancient history and the history of religions, not to mention a firm grasp of Latin, Greek and Hebrew.

My father was the first to withdraw from the Witnesses. He was a very quiet and reserved man; he had been spending as much time as he could in their fellowship and then suddenly this stopped, but he would not tell us why. Later we learned that they had tried to pressurize him into greater activity—even to give talks at the Thursday sessions (theological school), but this would have been quite out of character for him. When they failed to persuade him they became very hostile, and so he left them.

6

Winter

How long wilt thou forget me, O Lord? for ever?
how long wilt thou hide thy face from me?
(Psalm 13:1).

Although my father had left the Witnesses, my mother
and I became more and more keen, and joined in all
the activities of the society. Our main contact was still
the woman who visited our area, going from door to
door; she always seemed to appear at the right
moment. One day my mother, remembering the last
message we had received at a seance, asked her if she
knew a Rose Grove, or Grover, and to our amazement
she said, "Why, that's me! Grover was my maiden
name!" We told her about the spiritualist message, to
look out for a Rose Grove, or Grover, because she
would be a great help in our spiritual life; and here
she was, and truly it was she who was drawing us
towards a faith which, we were sure, was the right one.
She was greatly concerned that we had been led to her
by means of a satanic religion, but she finally
concluded that this was like Paul's experience in Acts
16:16-18.

Although I was keen on the work of witnessing I
was not happy; I often felt isolated and out of step
with everyone else, in my task of stressing the fear of
Armageddon; yet this is central to Witness teaching,
and the more I prayed for an alternative, the more
Armageddon was preached, and my confidence in myself was slipping away. As I looked back on those days
I realize how highly organized we were—like puppets,
dancing on strings that were pulled in America. We
spent all our time reading Watchtower publications.
The *Watchtower Magazine* was the basis for the Sunday
evening study, so that we read this carefully before the

meeting. "Have you read the latest *Watchtower*?" was the usual greeting, one to another. "Isn't it tremendous? Such prophecy! Wonderful!" Lamely I agreed. The continual harping on the destruction of Armageddon made me as sick as if I had seen a nasty accident, but they revelled in it, for they, Jehovah's true Witnesses, would see the annihilation of their enemies; they would have the victory; they would gain world rule! I was reading continually, too, of our Russian brothers and sisters being beaten and tortured and drugged until their personality was destroyed, and if they betrayed their faith they would thus be condemned by Jehovah. Their former faithfulness was all in vain, and they might as well have gone the way of the world from the beginning.

There was, as well, a continual fulmination against the Church, the medical profession, education, authority, Royalty, Government, and so on. *They* were wrong —*we* were right! I kept very busy with it all; on Sundays it was Kingdom Hall, studying the *Watchtower*; Tuesday evening was devoted to the study of another publication, after thorough preparation beforehand. On Thursday evenings there was a theological school, where the men were taught the art of public speaking, and we all studied the techniques of door-to-door work, so that we were all thoroughly prepared before we set out. It was extremely clever psychologically, and we knew what our "customers" reactions would be before we started talking. We needed, of course, to say who we were; but we had three or four aliases to catch people off their guard. We realized that many people, if they gathered at the outset who we really were, would slam the door in our faces! But when we used one of our aliases they would respond by telling us what they were, and we were able quite easily to draw the conversation round to our way of thinking. We practised the proper approach to the naive, the aggressive, the poor, the rich, the young, the aged; we were thoroughly schooled to tackle all characters. So we called ourselves members of the Watchtower Society, or the International Bible Students Association. Some merely said that they were missionaries. We only admitted that we *were* Jehovah

Witnesses if the person at the door challenged us with this.

I hated these Thursday meetings, dreading the time when I would be expected to take an active part, and I spent most of the time squirming down in my seat, trying to make myself shorter and thereby less noticeable. This was strange, for in the ordinary way I enjoyed any kind of platform speaking, but this simply did not appeal. On Wednesdays I followed my own studies with my uncle's landlady, an aged widow, ex-Salvation Army. Mondays, Fridays and Saturdays, although clear for personal matters, were in fact taken up with preparation—the following week's *Watchtower* commitments, and the door-to-door and street work which might follow. So busy! yet, without realizing it, living in the spirit of Philippians 3:6—"Concerning zeal, persecuting the church; touching the righteousness which is in the law, blameless". So busy! yet also lonely and right out of touch with my own age-group. There were indeed quite a few Jehovah Witness teenagers, but they were busied by the Society's demands.

We had to make reports on all our activities outside the Kingdom Hall—our comings and goings, our studies, our door-to-door work, publications sold, our back-calls; and all this was collated on a chart each month. All this can be confirmed from *Let God Be True* (see p. 222). This naturally spurred us on, for the previous month's totals had to be surpassed every time. It is amazing, too, how the spirit of competition keeps one on one's toes— and how fruitless my two hours looked when I had completed my report form. I seemed to have worked and studied so hard; I had attended all the meetings, but there seemed hardly a thing to put on this questionnaire! I never sold any publications; I never felt at home with the "sales-approach" talk, which was just like a TV commercial. There always seemed to be someone hovering around me when I was form-filling, and my efforts were often harshly criticized.

I often protested about all these forms. Surely Jehovah Himself knew what I had done, and that was enough? But Head Office kept an eagle eye on these routines, and were hot on the trail if the figures were down. So

29

we exaggerated our true figures so as to keep the smiles on the faces of the big-wigs! Despite all my zeal at this time, there seemed, unhappily, to be some invisible barrier which prevented me from making friendships, or feeling that I really belonged to the Society. I never made an intimate friend, and life seemed unbearable in isolation.

I did not feel led to make a stand in the waters of baptism, although I had the opportunity at a number of conventions at Wembley, Worthing, Hove and several other places. Baptism meant something more to me than being herded together and dipped in a public baths; I felt that there was something not quite right about it all, though as I never attended one of these occasions I cannot define what I really felt. I had always accepted believers' baptism, for Christ had begun His ministry by entering the river Jordan to be baptized by John the Baptist, and this was obviously the Father's will, since the Holy Spirit then descended upon Him, and the voice from heaven declared, "This is my beloved Son, in whom I am well pleased" (Matt. 3:17). Obviously Christ's action pleased His Father, and baptism was always in the mind of Christ and His disciples, and this was His last command before His ascension. But I couldn't imagine a glorious experience of the Holy Spirit coming at these immersions, for these did not mark an experience of believing in Christ as Saviour, but signalized the beginning of life as a minister in the Watchtower Society, and in this I could not feel I would be pleasing the Father or following in Christ's footsteps. In fact, however, I could not have put all this into words: I just didn't want to be baptized.

I was feeling very disappointed. Was I really expected to spend my life devoted to preaching fears of extreme persecution as prophesied in the Scriptures (namely, the Great Tribulation and, of course, Armageddon)? I had been promised missionary work if I joined them, and all they gave me was door-to-door work, in which I could not succeed, because I lacked the inner conviction that this demands. I rejected the idea of becoming a pioneer (one who follows ordinary part-time employment, and devotes the rest of his time to the Watchtower Organization), and I obtained a full-time post in an office when I left school. So much for my ambitions!

I was also very unfavourably impressed because at the start we were told that the Organization believed in faith-healing, but never, never did I see any. Why lie about this? It was not imagination, or a misunderstanding, for we had quite a discussion on the subject, and I was told that they believed in faith-healing. It had been a deliberate lie. Yet I tried to shrug it off; I was to learn to whitewash the Witnesses, and to persist in lying myself to cover up for them, in the years to come.

The months went by, but they seemed like years, for the Society is a hard task-master, and the isolation from the rest of the world was so real. But I didn't doubt the Society for one moment—one didn't! I didn't doubt the existence of Jehovah; of course He was Creator, and of course His Son lived on earth two thousand years ago, was crucified, rose again, and is now seated on the Father's right hand. I believed it all! A "born-again" Christian will observe that some of the most important fundamental principles of Christianity were missing from that confession of belief, but at that time I was too fast in the slavery of the Organization, and confused in intellectual respects. As I have said earlier, one needs a thorough grounding in early religions, and above all to be born again to prove that these beliefs are false. Anyone who reads *What has Religion done for Mankind?* will appreciate this.

A Christian believes that the power of prayer helps him in his day-to-day conflicts, but as Jehovah's Witnesses we believed that the only form of prayer acceptable to Him was "Thy will be done", which was to use us to help establish the Kingdom on earth by preaching the good news. Good news? What good news? I could see nothing good about our main theme—annihilation at Armageddon, and all the fears that went with it. Surely this is satan's work for, realizing he has such a short time to live, he is in fact convincing so many that their poor frail bodies can and will stand up to God's wrath at Armageddon, when the whole contour of the world will change, for they readily deny 1 Thess 4:17 and other supporting scriptures. Jesus promised escape as found in Luke 21:36.

The prayers at our meetings were very short, and only at the beginning; indeed, public prayer was regarded as hypocritical, and this was suported by Bible references like Luke 18:10-14 and Matthew 6:5-8, where there are instances of worthless prayers. However, in the quietness of my room I did pray—for a friend. I was so lonely, inwardly lonely; it was strange to be in an active fellowship, to be with people and yet feel lost. In my isolation I missed the companionship of my friends of former days. I was a teenager, alone: I should be gay, laughing, full of fun, not in this pit of darkness and despair. That was all I wanted—a friend.

A group of us had intended to spend a Bank Holiday Monday on the beach, but it poured with rain, and the others went to see a film—I, thinking that no one would turn up, had stayed indoors scowling at the deluge and feeling most disappointed. I was still depressed when I went to the next meeting, and heard them making arrangements for another outing on the following Saturday. They didn't notice me, and I knew I didn't belong. I sped home, and retreated to my bedroom, fighting back my bitter tears.

Why don't people leave the Witnesses when they get into this state of mind? Ah—if only it was as simple as that! Both William Schnell, author of *Thirty Years a Watchtower Slave*, and Ted Dencher, who wrote *Why I Left Jehovah's Witnesses*, found escape almost impossible. One becomes bound hand and foot to the Society; their mark is imprinted on one's forehead and right hand, one thinks and lives Watchtower Society. Ex-Jehovah Witnesses understand so perfectly the verses in the book of the Revelation, 13:16-17; for our "buying and selling" was closely watched and checked by the Society. Labour-saving devices might be approved, as leaving further time for door-to-door work, but the buying a car or a TV set, for example, was frowned on. These two adult and intelligent men, sane, with fully-developed personalities, had felt themselves entangled in this web without hope of escape; so what chance had I—a teenager who had only just left school!

It seems incredible that in the free western world there can be slavery and bondage so absolute, and worse than any physical imprisonment. No one can really appreciate the situation until he has experienced it. After all, where does anyone begin, if he starts to doubt the Organization, and wants to return to the outside world? Remember; the Watchtower Society had hitherto controlled all his life; the convert wipes his hands clean of family, friends, of everyone not associated with them. I want to emphasize the close similarity between the methods of the Organization and of the Nazis and the Communists. Much could be written on this score, but I shall be content if this parallel is borne in mind by my readers.

True, once before I had lived in a closed community, that of the convent—a life I could have loved, apart from being homesick. But throughout I was always being prepared for the day when I could leave the cloisters and enter the world again, and I was happy about this. But to enter the world again after being a Jehovah's Witness would be an admission of defeat in my hopes. Also it would be humiliating. We were so adamant to others; we were Jehovah's chosen, we had the monopoly of heaven and earth, and would rule after Armageddon. We were ready to jeer at Christians and at their Church and faith. We would do much to induce hostility and persecution, and would then turn smugly to texts like Matthew 5:11. How arrogant we were— the New World with Christ was ours!

We were certain that people who now refused "the truth" and who mocked us and scoffed, would, during Armageddon, clutch us by our clothing and cry to us "Why didn't you *make* us listen?" We, the chosen few, would have won Christ's Kingdom *via* Armageddon, and our chief enemy, the Church, with its priests, ministers and pastors, would not be spared. They were all twentieth-century scribes and pharisees, the successors of those who, two thousand years ago, had compassed Christ's death. Only fourteen at this time, I was taking it upon myself to instruct people very much my senior, in the ways of life and worship—and children are still doing this today. How then, could any Witness go back to such a world?

Our training could only be described as brainwashing; a regimented ideology drawn from the *Watchtower*, *Awake*, and other publications—to the exclusion of personal Bible reading, as depicted in John 5:39. There was no time for this; in any case, we were taught that the Bible could be approached with safety only through the Watchtower Society, because of its complexity, and because it had been for so long misinterpreted in Christendom. Nor was there any "quiet time": there seemed to be no ties between Jehovah and me. My prayers seemed to echo in space and return to me empty, void and unheard.

In addition to my spiritual conflict, home anxieties were taking their toll, for my mother was continually ill—a woman who had never had even a cold until the time when she asked help of a healer. She had always been as strong as a horse, but now with each passing month more of her energy and spirit was slipping away. I must confess that I was not much help after all she had done for me. My experiences seemed to have left me emotionally as hard as nails, and empty of all compassion. I looked upon her with pity, and felt sorry for her, but was powerless to lift a finger to help.

How many times have I heard this about Jehovah's Witnesses! and it is perfectly true. As a result of the continual brainwashing all appeals from others for help fall on deaf ears. Members of this sect are completely incapable of understanding human illnesses or anxieties. Once they also had the gift of laughter and tears, joy and sadness; but now they are merely mechanical zombies.

*   *   *

When we joined the Witnesses they were shocked, for we wore silver crucifixes round our necks. For us they were a testimony of our belief in Christ's salvation through His death on the cross. These were our first birthday gifts when my father came home from the war; in the long days of waiting for his return we said

34

that if he were returned to us safe, these were the presents we would ask him for, so that they meant a lot to us. But the Watchtower people demanded that we remove them; for they maintain that Christ was crucified upon a stake, with no cross-bar, with His arms above His head, and this is how all their illustrations show Him. In *The Kingdom is at Hand* (pp. 250-251) they have changed all the John 19 references, reading "stake" instead of "cross", and so through all their publications. (In the Society's *New World Translation of the Holy Scriptures* "stake" has been altered to "impale").

Jehovah's Witnesses opposed National Service. Certainly God may call some to be "conscientious objectors", though some older Witnesses tried to suggest that the best way for the young men concerned would be to report to the authorities and explain that they served Jehovah, and that His commands came first and foremost in their hearts and minds; but this humble and sensible method of seeking to withdraw from National Service and at the same time witnessing to one's faith was spurned by the hot-headed. They did great harm to the Movement by just disappearing— even succeeding in leaving the country—and altogether leading Caesar a proper dance; after which, if they were brought to court, they revelled in their claims of being "persecuted". Whenever Witnesses were taken to the tribunals their behaviour was abominable. They sought to disregard the magistrates completely, and if told to stand they ignored this on the grounds of Daniel 3. My mother, who attended one such case, was very surprised at the tolerance of the magistrates, clerks, police and all concerned. The Witnesses behaved like children revelling in misbehaviour. Ted Dencher says in his book "Wherever I went, I saw that Jehovah's Witnesses were expert at causing trouble". He wrote of America, and it was the same in England.

Having refused to stand at the entry of the magistrates into the court, their next strategy was to refuse to swear on any version of the Bible except their own. When all this resulted in frayed tempers, as was sometimes the case, the Witnesses took this as further evidence that they were being persecuted. Despite this behaviour, the English and American authorities were fair and lenient, and as I have already said, the older Witnesses did appreciate the Government's point of view, but they were not listened to. William Schnell mentions this disrespect for the older members in his book, and I saw this for myself. The others continued to claim that they were being persecuted, but any sympathy for them was misguided. The courts had spent many pounds and man-hours tracking down Witnesses who had disappeared around the time when their papers came through.

The claim for exemption from military service was based on the fact that they were Ministers of Jehovah, just as ministers of the Church were exempted. Very few Witnesses could properly claim such exemption, for very few were either pioneers or full time servants, and they had not undertaken theological training. One hour's study a week formed no real basis for their claims. Further, if they had been subjected to a written examination on Scripture to prove their claims, they would have lost hands down, because they did not read their Bibles! William Schnell's book confirms this.

Although at this time I saw life through Watchtower glasses, and faithfully observed the discipline, there were many questions in my mind. Had I been a man, what real arguments were contained in my copy of *Let God be True*, if I took it to the tribunal? It was folly to believe that passive resistance would bring world peace. God had led the Israelites into battle, and given them victory over the heathen: and the heathen regimes of the twentieth century must also be opposed in His name.

In the quiet of my room I would ask Jehovah to give me clear understanding, but confusion still filled my mind—and then I felt that this was from Satan. I seemed continually to be thinking on lines different from the Witness teaching. My mind was in a constant turmoil, with so many unanswered questions. By now I had lost the vision of a caring, loving, merciful Heavenly Father, in whom I had put my trust in earlier years. He had been replaced for me by a wrathful Jehovah God, a hard task-master, never satisfied. Yet all the time I might have turned to my Bible and been liberated through the precious name of the Lord Jesus Christ and received the spirit of adoption (Romans 8:15).

My deep-seated loneliness was recurring, and I took this problem to Jehovah, too. He had created Eve as a companion for Adam, saying, "It is not good that man should be alone; I will make him an help meet for him". I wasn't asking for a husband; just someone of my own age to talk to and laugh with, a friend, someone I could look forward to meeting, and going around with. Someone of either sex would do—surely this wasn't too much to ask, for the world is such a big place to travel on one's own! I seemed to have come to the end of my endurance, and I just couldn't take any more. Yet if I left the Watchtower Society, where else could I go? They declared that the Church doesn't care, and that the clergy could not care less about individuals. They could produce a lot of evidence for this, and people who were not Jehovah's Witnesses said the same. Time and again, when I was doing door-to-door work, I found people who had regularly attended a church for years, and had made it their life; and when something may have prevented them from attending they are faced with the hurtful realization that they haven't even been missed and that no one cares! The churches seem incapable of dealing with this situation, for when people feel abandoned and sore, it is the Jehovah's Witnesses who step into the breach and appear like angels sent from God. They do pride themselves on calling on their people if they don't attend the meetings; all comings and goings are noted, and absentees are quickly followed up.

It is the same in America; Ted Dencher says "Jehovah's Witnesses find many people who have a gripe against their church", and again, "some persons feel neglected within the Church. They want attention and no one seems to be giving it to them. Then along comes a Jehovah's Witness, who appears to be keenly interested in them, and who showers them with attention." But as one who had all the Watchtower Society doctrines at my finger tips, it was perturbing to find that I didn't belong anywhere at all. One particular Saturday evening, still feeling very low in spirit, I saw my Jehovah's Witness comrades, who were out for the evening. They didn't see me, and I purposely watched them from a distance; they were laughing and talking loudly and cheerfully, and *I knew that I didn't belong*.

7

Winter Continues

But they made light of it, and went their ways,
one to his farm, another to his merchandise.
(Matthew 22:5).

Two out and one to go—even then I could not believe
that the Watchtower was anti-christ. It was obvious
that I had not been chosen like Paul, in his letter to
the Galatians (1:15) "But when he who had set me
apart before I was born, and had called me through
his grace..."; I had not been elected by Jehovah to
work for Him; my services were not required. He had
withdrawn Himself and would not even listen to my
prayers. I had stumbling-blocks in my path, as big as
mountains. I had to accept that I was not one of the
elect among the number to make up the Kingdom. I
had tried so hard and believed so much, and as I found
that I was rejected and cast aside with the rabble for
destruction, there was only one thing left—to join the
rabble. This greatly concerned my mother, and does
to this day. But I entered into "the world" with all its
entertainments—dancing, cinemas, making friends, joining a church youth club. As time went by I wondered
what all the point had been about "withdrawing from
the world", for I found the world far less evil than the
cutting tongues of the Watchtower Society. True, I
now rubbed shoulders with some who revelled in mis-
conduct of various kinds, but I didn't have to join in
with them. I knew right from wrong, and I knew the
consequences of doing wrong, and these things helped
me to hold to my principles. I could begin to see so
clearly why Christ loved the sinners and condemned
some of the "righteous". I found real happiness with
my new friends and went along with them in great
relief. I had rejected "the Kingdom", the brethren but

not their teachings for subconsciously I retained them: I was convinced that their kingdom would be worse than hell, with all the do's and don'ts of a harsh cruel God. But though I had left the Watchtower Society I had not reached any new and positive beliefs, and I still fell back on their doctrines in debates and discussions. I had tried to be done with it all, but these things remained ingrained. My friends called me controversial, and sometimes cynical.

Having joined the youth club I was committed to church attendance, but it had lost its meaning. Actually I enjoyed going, and it was the right thing to do, but it was only superficial.

By this time my mother was very ill and was in great need of medical attention. But the fear of blood transfusion led her to refuse hospital treatment. She got weaker and weaker; it was terrible to watch her shrivel away, practically to a lifeless corpse. Yet, realizing that she might need blood, and that they would insist on transfusion, she continued to refuse an operation. Not once did she waver; she would sooner die, if necessary! It is impossible to put into words the mental agony we went through. There was no comfort anywhere; there was certainly no comfort in her religion, but just the nagging command "No blood! no blood!" We had promised to honour her belief, but we were fearful lest she should die; her strength was diminishing. One Saturday I came home from work. She was weak and frail, her face a yellow waxen mask; she didn't even look human. How much longer must we watch this slow torturing illness gnawing away at her?

She asked me something so simple—just to cook the cabbage. I can't explain my conduct, but I just shouted "Put the cabbage on yourself! I'm not going to lift a finger to help you! I expect my meals to be on the table when I come home from work, and the house clean. Do you realize the doctors are ready and waiting to help you, and you won't let them? You're trying to commit suicide. Call yourself a Jehovah's witness? You won't do much witnessing six foot underground. Look at you now—useless to God and man! All right, die! Have you ever thought of the

40

people you're leaving behind? Make a marvellous story, that will—that God decreed that you should suffer to the end, and we watched it and lived to tell of His love and compassion to us! I can see people pouring into the Kingdom Hall on the strength of that! Come on—get up and get my dinner!" This outburst of fury and sarcasm at least relieved my feelings—of course, it was prompted (even if not excused) by my deep anxiety.

It wasn't long afterwards that she was admitted to hospital for the necessary operation. After seeing her so ill, I dreaded my first visit after the operation. We got there early and hung about the corridors. As I fought back my tears, I felt that I hadn't the strength to see more suffering. But to my amazement, instead of being weak after her ordeal, she was sitting up in bed, as bright as a button! I could have cried with sheer relief. The operation had only been a minor one, and blood transfusion had not been needed.

During the last three years my mother had changed. I assumed that this was the result of her long-drawn out illness, which was bound to leave mental and physical scars, and one needed patience and endurance to cope with it. I didn't realize that her trouble was the result of this religion—its teachings and doctrines and books, which prohibited any contact with those outside the Organization. During her illness mother spent most of her time reading Watchtower literature. She had a good brain and absorbed knowledge like blotting-paper. Her confinement at home prevented her meeting other people or having outside interests; she was virtually a prisoner surrounded by propaganda, without an anti-dote, and just drinking in the poison, undiluted. By then I had no knowledge at all of what was behind the covers of the books she studied. I hardly realized that although I had left the Organization, my life was still being shaped by the Watchtower. I kept hoping that her manner towards us would improve with her health, and patiently we waited—tomorrow, to-morrow!

Our home was now an impersonal place for eating, shelter and sleeping; it had nothing of the atmosphere of home—it was cold, hard and loveless. This was so noticeable when I visited friends in their homes, and I knew companionship, and, above all, a warm welcome. Visitors were not welcome in ours; they were inferior and of the devil, even if it wasn't put quite so bluntly as that. I tried to avoid bringing new friends home (the old ones were oblivious to it all). It was very embarrassing, especially with boy-friends; I had to say a quick "good-night", and dash indoors to avoid making excuses about not asking them in. It was frustrating and heart-breaking, to meet on street corners, or outside cinemas and dance halls. Sometimes arrangements had to be broken. It looked to them as though I wasn't keen, and had tried to stop them calling on me. I couldn't explain; one doesn't criticise parents or lower their image before others. It was evident that I had outstayed my welcome in my home. How I envied my friends who lived in real homes, and how I wished I could be proud of mine! But when mother's health returned everything would be different, I was sure. Meantime I tried to behave nonchalantly, but all the while I was suffering embarrassment, repression and disappointment, as friends left me, all because our front door had become an iron curtain.

At this time mother was baptized at a convention. I would not answer when she spoke about it, let alone be a spectator. I had always believed in adult baptism, but this seemed to have little or no spiritual meaning, for there was no God for us any more. He had withdrawn His hand, ages before.

Nothing that I could do or say could stop it, but I knew that she was not being baptized into God's ordinance. She tried to win me back into "the truth" by argument and through prayer, but I became the more determined not to be swayed. She reprimanded me, and quoted Scripture at me—"In the last days children shall be disobedient to their parents" (Rom. 1:30, 2 Tim 3:2), but this only aroused resistance on my part.

One evening I got home rather late, and went in to say goodnight to my parents. My father was not yet in bed, but I found mother there, looking so frail and tired, the enormous double bed emphasizing her small-ness. She said, "Will you read the Bible to me? My eyes are so tired." Like an animal fearing the snare, I fought and struggled. "Listen, I've been through all that once; you're not getting me on that lark again!"

"My eyes are tired, and I can't see." Anger surged within me. "Well," I said angrily, "Get yourself some glasses! they're free on the National Health!" and I left the room as fast as I could.

8

Prospects of Spring

Wherefore comfort yourselves together. (1 Thess. 5:11).

Things got better between my mother and me when I met the man I was to marry. We had been going together for quite a short time when he penetrated that iron curtain front door. He just called and they let him in; it was as simple as that! I feared further domestic scenes, but to my surprise family relationships improved during the next few months, and everything in the garden was lovely, as it had been years before.

We got engaged on my birthday, and my family gave us a lovely party; but our happiness was short-lived, and we were soon in trouble. My fiancé and I were subjected to sheer unadulterated hatred, and our engagement, instead of being enjoyable, with a sense of growing love, became simply hell on earth. The front door became an iron curtain again, and we were told that we could meet at the bottom of the road—rain, shine, snow or sleet. We spent the next fifteen months trying to survive continual nagging and scolding. After six months of this I decided to break off the engagement. Obviously the prospect of my marriage was distressing my mother, and perhaps I was being selfish. Once again her health was deteriorating. But then I told myself that I had the right to decide my own future, and here was a man who seemed ready to take more than his fair share of difficulties, and be for me a rock, a foundation. So I apologized, and we came together again.

The winter months were the worst, having to meet in the cold, and sometimes walking around in the rain if the car wouldn't go, and have a coffee somewhere, and then home again wet and freezing. Cafes and public houses were our refuge, and they gave us warmth, shelter and companionship. Cinemas and dance halls also provided entertainment as well as temporary consolation.

Several times I considered leaving home altogether. I knew that my fiancé's family would welcome me; but I tried at all costs to stay with my parents. We had been through too much in the past to make a break. But though I couldn't think of life without them, the immediate future looked grim. Early in November I was taken ill with bronchitis. I had walked about with it for days before giving up the fight and going to bed. There followed weeks of isolation; no visitors, just the long, long days. Without fail he would call, and I heard muffled voices at the front door. All day I had longed for this visit; all day I tried to will that I might be allowed just this one visitor. But there was a very brief conversation downstairs, and then the door shut and I heard footsteps; my bedroom door opened and my father brought in some present from him. Cold comfort! and another twenty-four hours would pass in the same way. I was too miserable to cry, but something very deep inside would ache. The more distressed I felt, too, the more my temperature would rise! so the situation became a vicious circle.

He wrote to me, of course, and I'm afraid that I didn't appreciate the love and the thoughtfulness behind this; for a person who hates writing even his signature, this was a great achievement! but I found letters a very poor substitute. The days dragged by and turned into weeks, and at last I recovered and was out by the weekend. How difficult it was to remain loyal to my parents! I had to lie and say that it was *I* who hadn't wanted visitors ... or that they thought it wise ... I felt that their honour was in my hands. Soon after that, history repeated itself, and I lost my job again. Mother was still pursuing her Bible studies with the aid of Watchtower books—in practice it was the other way round. But this certainly didn't bring any love into our home. I often thought about this. We had been a happy family once, but suddenly we weren't any more. We were like foreigners who could not understand each other's language. When had it started, this breaking apart? Really, there was only one answer, and I reached it every time—it dated from the time when we joined the Jehovah's Witnesses. But like an ostrich burying its head in the sand I couldn't see this. I put the blame in every quarter except the right one. I couldn't believe that they could possibly cause such misery to others not of their faith, and use Jehovah's name while they did this.

I could not use Scripture in my arguments; I didn't know where to find appropriate texts, and anyway they will not accept other people's interpretations of Scripture. Their way of using the Word of God makes it into a sword which only harms and maims and brings hatred between people, and that surely makes the Bible contradict itself. I got to feel sick when I saw a Bible lying around, at the thought that so much anguish could come from reading it and acting upon what was read. So I made excuses for my mother—her illness, her change of life, her weariness after the long years spent caring for me with my asthma. I took care that no one should realize that she was a Witness, for surely she was an exception to the rule. I still believed in the integrity of the Watchtower Society. True, I had left, but this was because I could not maintain the very high standard of living that Jehovah required—it was I that was wrong. They claimed that they were Jehovah's Witnesses, working heart and soul for Him; and their work can and does put many churches to shame. Surely it was inconceivable that so much work, zeal and study was not of God?

*　　*　　*

Trouble about my proposed marriage was inevitable; from a Jehovah's Witness point of view my husband-to-be was of the devil, and would provoke the persecution written of in Matt. 10:21 and 24:10. As a Jehovah's Witness, therefore, mother must make every endeavour to stop our marriage. *This Means Everlasting Life* says:

Continuing to live with an unbelieving mate may subject the believing one to trialsome disagreeableness at home or to some form of domestic persecution.

46

From her standpoint, mother genuinely had my welfare at heart. Married to an unbeliever, I would never get through Armageddon; I was lost. I was not honouring my parents, as written in Ephesians 6:1. The whole point of this situation can be seen in 2 Cor. 6:14 (RSV) "Do not be mismated with unbelievers. For what partnership have righteousness and iniquity? Or what fellowship has light with darkness? What accord has Christ with Belial? Or what has a believer in common with an unbeliever?" I argued on another text—one of the few I did know, 1 Cor. 7:14, "For the unbelieving husband is consecrated through his wife", and (v. 16) "Wife, how do you know whether you will save your husband?" 1 Peter 3:1, "Likewise, you wives, be submissive to your husbands, so that some, though they do not obey the word, may be won without a word by the behaviour of their wives, when they see your reverent and chaste behaviour" (RSV).

On the other hand, we had only two more years to go before Armageddon (that was in 1957), so why undertake such a venture now? (Matt. 12:39 and 16:4 rebuke those who look for signs.) All the more reason why I should marry him and pray for his conversion. I prayed for a conversion like Paul's, for nothing is impossible to God! But I was answered by page 219 of *Let God be True*, which says, "Indeed they recognize that it is impossible to convert the wicked and ungodly". Paul does advise the Corinthians against marrying an unbeliever, but *This Means Everlasting Life* suggests in the section on Marriage among the Heirs of Life that marriage should be avoided even by believers, as Paul advises in 1 Cor. 7:8-9. We read (p. 147)

The person that marries takes on a responsibility, therefore, that fences in his personal freedom and he takes on the most intimate care of life-long mate. Because a Christian marriage cannot be dissolved by divorce except if one of the mates proves unfaithful, it is a matter for sober thought whether a single Christian who wants to be a preacher of good news as freely and as fully as possible should marry or re-marry.

On occasions Jehovah's Witness parents refuse their

consent to a marriage, and the young people have either taken the matter to court or flitted to Scotland. But in any case I was no longer a Jehovah's Witness, so why should I be bound by their beliefs? Ted Dencher also had this experience, for he writes, "The current 'party line' when I came in was, 'Don't get married— Armageddon is right round the corner'. It seemed that marriage might somehow cramp one's style, or spoil one's chance of getting through Armageddon alive!"

It seems to me that the Watchtower Society had misconstrued Paul's advice on celibacy. There can be very few people who have been given the call to undertake this high vocation. Admittedly, matrimonial ties would of course be a great hindrance to one who had been given a spiritual family to nurture. But this must be a matter for individuals; it is surely wrong to impose such a burden upon all. It would deny the human comfort which is to be found in matrimonial partnership.

My parents saw no point in my prayers for my fiancé's conversion; they just didn't appreciate my faith in the power of God. But surely it is right to ask God for His gifts, and Luke 18 confirms this. We should beat on the gates of heaven until our prayers are answered; we are to pray unceasingly, and not to faint. Then we should give the Father the praise and glory.

The months passed slowly, and we named the wedding day. Financially this was suicide, for we hadn't saved much. I had been out of work time and time again with bronchitis. We had saved as much as we could, but only after indulging in our pleasures. My fiancé said "We don't know what is before us, and we might as well look back later on, and say, 'Well, we did have a good time when we were young!'" But only God knew what was in store for us.

For me there was the problem—Church or Registry Office? I still retained enough of the Witness outlook not to want a church wedding. First, I felt that such a ceremony with its pomp, and the use of a church to show off my pretty dress, was hypocritical to say the least. Then, like the Witnesses, I deplored the policy of clergy who permitted their churches to be used for christenings, weddings and funerals with no other attendances in between. This permitted people to use God and His Church, just keeping up old customs without any thought of why they were there and of the promises that they would have to make. With most people it seemed to be a matter of "get this lot over and get on with the drinking!" The drinking was the god for many of them, so why not perform the ceremony where their god was?

This Means Everlasting Life goes on to say that one should be married by an officer of the law of the land and have the marriage legally acknowledged, and that there are no biblical references to priests or clergymen being needed to complete a marriage. *Let God be True* and other Watchtower publications reject the world and its man-made rules, holding that the devil is the invisible ruler of the world. Ted Dencher says "The Society teaches that all earthly governments are of the Devil. This causes the Witness to lose all respect for civil authority," and thus there is no need for even a civil ceremony. I have often known of Witnesses being accused of immorality and loose living, but I have heard of only a few cases of adultery—and these people have been ejected from the Society.

With such ideas, how could I possibly go into a church? I could not tell my fiancé all this, and say why I wanted a registry office wedding; and I was surprised when he just said, "No church—no wedding!" and he was adamant! And so it was that although I had lost my faith in Christ and the Church, this issue became something of a turning-point for me, and while my thoughts were still not very clear, I was once again certain of God and of His power and I wanted my wedding to be within His will and to have His blessing.

9

A new Day will bring Happiness

Marriage is honourable in all. (Hebrews 13:4).

From the point of view of my former associates I had really gone to the devil and must be treated with the contempt I deserved. But in any case I was now due for demolition at Armageddon anyway. The happiness and excitement of my wedding preparations were utterly spoiled by the atmosphere at home, and I just didn't know what any day might bring.

In the past my parents had been talking about moving into smaller accommodation when I married, then suddenly all conversation of this nature stopped as though it had been a passing fad, there was no further indication of intentional move until one day I nearly fell over the carpets right in my way. I swore, and demanded to know what was going on. "Nothing— they are going to be cleaned." That wanted some believing; yet surely we couldn't be moving? Naturally they would tell me about that, and packing would have started already. Yet a few days later, when I was about to rush out of the house in my usual early morning mad panic, I was told, "Don't come back here this evening; we're moving to..." (an address in another town).

Many people could not believe this at the time, and many will question it now, but it is absolutely true. It was typical of Witnesses to expose unbelievers to as much inconvenience as possible to prove their own superiority. All the arrangements for my wedding had to be altered. The removal lengthened my travelling time to and from work very considerably, and gave me a day of eleven or twelve hours. I got absolutely tired out, and living in the new home, in a rural area, on a building site full of dust and reeking with paint, brought back my asthma in full power. Then my parents refused to sign the form of consent (I was eight months under twenty-one). In any case, they told me that they would not come to the wedding; my mother even made arrangements to be out of the country, but made a mistake in the date. We faced the unhappy prospect of going to court to appeal, and I didn't want the publicity of that. My parents took my insistence on getting married, and my disobedience to them, as confirmation of the signs of the times, as revealed in such scripture passages as Micah. 7:6, Matthew 10:21, 35-36, Mark 13:12, Luke 12:53 and 2 Tim 3:1-5; and their tactics would seem to them to be justified by the passage in *This Means Everlasting Life* (p. 249):

Hence parents need to be specially mindful of God's commandments that concern the lasting good of their offspring. They need to fight the world tendency and put up a hard fight for the faith once for all time delivered to the holy ones by doing their utmost to rear their children aright.

Later in the same chapter, Proverbs 23:13 is quoted: *"Withhold not correction from the child: for if thou beatest him with the rod he shall not die. Thou shalt beat him with the rod, and shalt deliver his soul from hell (sheol)."* This mention of the "rod of correction" that is used to turn the children from the way of death in disobedience to God does not need to be a literal stick. The rod symbolizes parental authority and power, and applying the "rod of correction" means for parents to exercise the power and authority entrusted to them in whatever way may seem Scripturally wise and suitable to correct the child. The parents' grip on the rod of power, authority and responsibility should never be relaxed, and respect for it should be impressed upon the young mind and heart. Such use of the rod for their lasting good does not spell brutality and oppression, but spells a parental love combined with wisdom and with godly strength. In the benefits resulting *later the corrected child will open its eyes to the wisdom and loving kindness of its earthly caretakers and will respect them for the more faithful correction. During correction it has the opportunity to show obedience and so learn in a most impressional manner the proper respect for God-given authority Thus it will learn to fear God and his supreme authority also. (Hebrews 12:9-11).*

The following chapter, "Surviving This World's End" (pp. 258-59) quotes Luke 17:26-30, "And as it was in the days of Noah, so shall it be also in the days of the Son of Man. They did eat, they drank, they married wives, they were given in marriage until the day that Noah entered into the ark, and the flood came, and destroyed them all. Likewise also as it was in the days of Lot; they did eat, they drank, they bought, they sold, they planted, they builded. But on the same day that Lot went out of Sodom it rained fire and brimstone from heaven and destroyed them all. Even thus shall it be in the day when the Son of Man is revealed." The people of Noah's day showed their lack of interest in his message and in the signs of the times by their normal conduct of eating and drinking, marrying and building.

I was amazed by my parents' attitude at the time, and much puzzled; but I can now see clearly that it was these scriptures and the Watchtower literature which influenced them. About six weeks before the wedding I found work nearer home. I didn't worry much about the sort of job; the wages were good, and it was pretty close to home. I did the necessary office-work of a shop, and also went behind the counter, dusted the stock and kept it in order. The dusting was rather thankless, for the shop was on a main road, but I enjoyed it, even if the shelves and the goods were bright and shining for only five minutes. But within a week or so I felt very unwell, and this got worse. Every day I hoped that I might feel better tomorrow, and that my asthma would subside. But I had to have the doctor, and he declared that it came from my new employment, and gave me a real wigging for getting a job that was hopeless for an asthmatic. When I explained that it was only a "fill-in" until my wedding, he said, "Well, that's off, for a start!" Everything was against us! I had only my will power.

But strangely, my mother became two women. Often I found her the mother who had brought me up in such love and care and kindness; and so the consent-form was signed without further ado. When during these last few weeks the Watchtower mask was removed, a rather excited parent was revealed, who evidently wanted to enjoy the wedding of her only child. She brought two dresses for herself, and revelled in getting my gown and the bridesmaids' gowns, touring the shops with a zeal which I found rather hard going on my feet! So I might meet one of two people—a mother or a Jehovah's Witness; one who loved me, or one who hated; a woman filled with excitement, or indifference, with enthusiasm or with opposition. It was not that she suffered from schizophrenia; she had been so brain-washed by this sect in every part of life that her strug-gles to enter real life again were opposed by what she had absorbed from them. A beatnik or drug-addict will know her situation exactly.

Many times she said, "I do want you to get married; of course I want your happiness," and this sounded quite sincere. But then she would add "But Armageddon is only just round the corner—only another two years. Why not wait?" (Of course, Matthew 24:36 shows Jesus saying, "Of that day and hour knoweth no man, no, not the angels of heaven, but my Father only").

One day when I was in my bedroom I overheard mother talking to a Witness friend, and telling her all her fears. This woman said, "Then you'll just have to pray about it, 'Thy will be done'." Those few words were like sunshine after a storm. Surely this woman was a Christian! I was so encouraged by this that for the first time I told my fiancé that my family was a Jehovah's Witness family—though it seemed like confessing that one was a teenage were-wolf! We went to a meeting at the local Kingdom Hall, and they gave us a warm welcome, but it did not grip us.

The behaviour of my family and myself was by now considered odd by relatives and friends who did not understand our theology; they were upset and puzzled. But for me the prospect of a new life lay ahead; yet how would my controversial attitudes fit in with adult responsibilities?

10

Caught

Holding the form of religion, but denying the power of it. Avoid such people. For among them are those who make their way into households and capture weak women, burdened with sins and swayed by various impulses. (2 Tim. 3:5-6) (RSV).

The long bitter years were gone, but they had left deep scars on my heart and mind. Finding myself now as a young wife in a new home came as a startling reality. The struggle of the past six years was over, but it had left me physically and mentally weary. Some sort of psychological reaction set in, and I spent the first four or five months suffering from severe depression. I wept and wept; I cried myself to sleep; I just burst into tears in the street or in a shop—anywhere and everywhere, and the whole situation was extremely embarrassing. My poor husband thought I was "acting the goat" and the doctor did his best to help me cure myself without going to hospital. But I felt so very ill; I wanted a refuge, a haven away from the harsh cruel world—indeed, I wanted to die.   All my strength had gone, and I was about as lifeless as a rag doll. I had a great fear of meeting people and would shake from head to foot if they appeared to have a dominant character. As for my husband, he terrified me! I ought to have realized that this was shock reaction, the past catching up with the present, but I could only think of the present, and my trouble must have come through to him. The months dragged by; I lived in hell, and no one understood.

The minister of the church where we had been married tried very hard to help, and I was grateful for his kindness. But it all seemed to be to no avail; there was so deep a cancer, which only time could heal.

This was the time when Russia started sending sputniks into space. So what the Witnesses were saying was true; by penetrating into the heavens in this manner they would bring down the wrath of God upon us. Russia would rule the world from space—and then Armageddon. They *were* right.

I wasn't left to brood over this for very long before a Witness called, a friend from my early days. She was more than ready and willing to explain Jehovah's intentions for the world. Who could dispute that this was a messenger from God? How strange it was! I had fought against this sect for so long, and now here I was sitting on the fence, not only eager to listen but ready to be pulled over. Further, it was my duty to join them now, for I had the added responsibility of my husband's salvation on my hands, since I knew the truth. To deny my allegiance to that truth would mean that I was causing his death. He would surely die, and I would be the murderer!

They won! Of course, I was in no state to argue as I might have done if only I myself had been involved; but I could not withstand the argument which concerned my husband—and remember, we had been married only a few weeks. I did not speak of my newly-recovered beliefs to anyone outside the home; subconsciously I was ashamed about it. Further, I didn't want to have anyone seeking to persuade me otherwise—for what else had they to offer?

One afternoon when a Watchtower book study was in progress, there was a call by the minister who had married us. Knowing that he would be like a red rag to a bull to the Jehovah's Witness, I ushered him into the kitchen. As we sat together there I perceived the reality of his ministerial vocation, to care for people. Whoever needed comfort and guidance and the hand of compassion would find them there. That minister's very presence and concern reminded me of the wonderful love and care of Jesus and His disciples for the sick, because they understood human frailties.

When he had gone, I told the Witness why he had come, but she charged me very plainly to expect salvation at Armageddon, looking neither to the left nor to the right. We must not be side-tracked and think of our present needs. Cold comfort! The only hope of the world is Armageddon, because this will abolish satanic rule once and for all, to deny that hope can only maintain Satan's power, and this seemed a powerful argument. After this incident the Witnesses called on this minister during their door-to-door visitations, and she brought me all sorts of discreditable tales about him. They are certainly experienced in mud-slinging and in making it stick, and few can escape their evil tongues.

I did not know at that time that my breakdown was something which often occurs among the Witnesses, and Ted Dencher says that some members were committed to institutions. I had often wondered what the Witnesses did about the mentally sick, since in their eyes doctors and psychiatrists are part and parcel of the satanic control of the world—particularly the latter, whom they really spurn with venom, mainly, I suspect, because psychiatrists tended to blame this religion for these breakdowns, and so tried to dissuade their patients from remaining in the Organization. But where then were the sick to go for treatment? They could not even call on Christ as the Supreme Physician, since, not believing in His true deity, they leave Him upon His throne with the sole task of preparing bowls of wrath for Armageddon.

However, the minister joined forces with my doctor, and between them they seemed to make a spiritual archway and in next to no time my health took a turn for the better, without medical or spiritual aid.

As a newly-married couple the subject of birth-control arose for us. The Witnesses disapprove of bringing children into this Satan-ridden world, for the little ones will be in the thick of Armageddon. But just as I had been determined to get married, with or without their approval, I was also determined to have children, and we moved to another flat, which would be convenient with an increase in family. Jehovah's Witnesses have an extremely good system of follow-up; one hasn't finished unpacking when they are at the door with a welcome into the new district, and giving

57

details of the whereabouts of the Kingdom Hall. This is certainly a point in their favour—and a note for the churches; there are no lost sheep here!

To my horror, I was found at the ante-natal clinic to be of the rhesus negative blood-group, and had to carry a green card in case of an accident. Obedient to Witness practice, I wrote on the bottom of my card "No blood to be given"; one must believe in all the doctrines of faith, and not pick out the agreeable parts. We were out to please God, not man. I was deeply concerned about this matter, more for my husband's point of view than mine. I kept trying to put myself in his shoes: I had watched my mother as she all but died in front of my eyes, or so it had appeared, and now I was submitting him to the possibility of the same ordeal—a far greater ordeal, in fact, for he might see two suffer, and maybe die. The situation was more difficult because I was given very precise details of authenticated cases where both mother and baby had been taken with disease through some accident or error during the transfusion process; indeed the patient might easily die. Otherwise, various psychological and mental results might be expected. They did not scruple to play upon one's fear of these physical and mental results of an incorrect transfusion; and for many, such fears could be more powerful even than fears of God's punishment for disobedience to His laws. They stressed that anyone who was restored to health by blood transfusion would in any case lose his life when Armageddon came. At times I felt strong disagreement with all their teaching, but Watchtower members have little chance to withstand the continual flood of literature, which prevents them from taking one point at a time, dealing just with this and then going on to another. The master-brains behind this organization have a thorough insight into the working of the human brain and mind.

The scripture supporting their beliefs about blood include Deut. 12:16, Lev. 7:26-27 and Acts 15:20, though it can soon be seen that these texts refer to sacrifices to God, to a dietary issue, or to a matter of forbidden pagan rituals and Satan-worship, for even in this twentieth century the shedding and drinking of blood, and blood sacrifices are still important in black magic. The texts have no reference to medical aspects. Since my day, however, the authorities have taken the matter to the courts, and although parents may have regretted this infringement of their authority they are in fact greatly relieved that the responsibility is no longer theirs.

My husband's opinions were more sane and logical than mine. Even if some might question the receiving of blood from a stranger, parents do in fact give their blood within the complex of making new life, so that the child may be of the same blood group as his father, and the mother of course by means of the continual flow of blood throughout her pregnancy. The parents who were the donors of blood in the first instance may surely repeat this gift later on. But the Watchtower answer to that argument was a definite refusal. The official line is to deprecate discussion of the subject as objectless—why prolong life when we must all die sooner or later? But there is surely room to enjoy what we may! Since I was extremely fit and well at the time, the matter did not cause me great concern, but since it was bound to be difficult if it did arise, I laid it before God in prayer.

One brilliantly sunny day a young Jehovah's Witness girl and I were on our way to an area allotted to us for door-to-door visiting. We laughed and chatted as we went; it was a glorious day and it seemed good to be alive. We had called at one or two houses, and then for me the faces of the people who answered the door began to turn into a grey swirl and then everything turned to blackness. I could not see a thing, and seemed to have been struck blind. I could not speak, either; my throat seemed paralysed. But directly the door was shut, I could see and speak again. We went to the next house, and the same thing happened. I was utterly at a loss; my colleague, not realizing what had happened, took my silence as a cue for her to do the talking. Then I told her what was happening and we tried to laugh it off; but it happened again, and finally I was reduced to sitting on a wall while she completed the houses in the road. How strange for this to take place! for I was carrying out Jehovah's work. But evidently this work was not for me. I did not understand why, but was not prepared to take risks of an accident, for each door had a short flight of steps leading up to it, and a stumble during one of these attacks might have caused a nasty fall, bringing hurt to my precious burden as well as myself.

I was loth to give up this work but did so, though the Witness leaders did not sympathize with my position, or the trouble which would result should I be involved in an accident. As far as I can remember they simply washed their hands of me.

*   *   *

Since my marriage my mother had found herself a job, but this was utterly condemned by Watchtower standards. *Let God be True* (p. 224) indicates the position:

> *He does not privately profit according to worldly standards of finance or social prestige upon becoming one of Jehovah's Witnesses. Indeed, he must divorce himself from all such standards and worldly ambitions in order to become one of Jehovah's Witnesses and to grow in favour with Almighty God (John 15:18-21). But because one of Jehovah's Witnesses gains no worldly or temporal advantage does not mean that he personally receives no benefit upon becoming one of Jehovah's Witnesses.*

> *While from a material standpoint God promises to His faithful servant only his daily bread and bare necessities of life . . .*

the passage goes on to speak of "spiritual blessings" and of the great privilege of being an ambassador for Almighty God and for His everlasting Theocratic government.

As my father was the bread-winner, mother should on no account take on employment, apart from serving the Watchtower Society, and that, of course, unpaid. Observance of this rule kept some Witnesses in real poverty. But since we say in the Lord's Prayer "Give us this day our daily bread", that is all we must expect, and nothing more; thereby when one enters the Society one also makes a vow of poverty. However, my mother's working days were brief, because her health failed again, so we joined forces and waited patiently for the new arrival which was to grace our home.

II

A Babe is Born

Suffer little children to come unto me, and forbid them not: for of such is the kingdom of God. (Luke 18:16).

I was delivered of a son, a lovely boy, but I felt too tired and exhausted to appreciate him. Things had gone extremely well until the later stages of labour. I knew the meaning of Genesis 3:16—"in sorrow thou shalt bring forth children". They gave me injections, but these seemed to accentuate the pain rather than assuage it. I do not know whether it was the injections, but at this time I had a terrible sense of all that Jehovah's Witness brothers and sisters were suffering in the Communist states, without any comforter or guide, and with no Christ. Even when as a child I was ill, in pain or undergoing something unpleasant, I would always pray for the Lord's presence to sustain me, and He in His mercy would soften the affliction; but now it seemed that I must undergo this without His help, and I could find no rest or peace of mind. I talked to Witnesses about this; they told me plainly, and brought Scripture to confirm it, that misery and travail and pain were all I could expect in childbirth; it was presumptuous to think otherwise. But my faith led me to believe that God's sovereign power could alter all that.

When we came proudly home with our new-born son we immediately encountered another obstacle; we were given a week's notice to quit our flat. We had taken the flat with baby in mind, but unfortunately there had been a change of landlords, and the new owner had different ideas about babies from those of the previous owner. It turned out that he had delayed the notice in case anything happened to the baby—in which case we might have stayed on.

We had now become a "Cathy Come Home" family. Local Councillors tried to persuade him to let us stay for six weeks while our own home was building, but he was adamant, and we had to go. We found some makeshift rooms, but it all spoiled our happiness. I felt guilty at bringing our baby into the world. The Jehovah's Witnesses could well have said "We told you so—we warned you!", but they didn't. However, after a week or two in our temporary abode, while I felt miserable and was wallowing in self-pity, a young Jehovah's Witness woman came to see me. We had heard of each other through our families, but had never met, but now, living in the same area, we could be friends. Surely this was an angel sent from heaven, and I was delighted to see her.

12

Home at Last

*And the rain descended, and the floods came,
and the winds blew, and beat upon that house; and
it fell not: for it was grounded upon a rock.*
(Matthew 7:25).

Two days before Christmas 1958 we moved into our
newly-completed bungalow, and despite the time of
year the weather was kind to us. How huge a three-
bedroom bungalow appeared after our two small furnished rooms! The sparse furniture we had looked lost
in it, and we could not imagine what it would look like
when each room was carpeted and furnished. But
that seemed a dream which might never come true.
However, I had the luxury of being able to turn the
taps on! and *hot* and cold water would run from them,
and one could wash up, do the washing and all such
chores without having to carry water from the landlady's kitchen or from the tap in the toilet, depending
whether I needed hot or cold water. We no longer had
to share a kitchen, either, and then carry the cooked
food up a flight of stairs.

The friendship mentioned in the previous chapter
did not last very long; once my husband and I had settled in our new home, she and I started a Bible Study;
but both being much the same age and each with
young babies, we found it tempting to talk about the
babies instead of concentrating on the real purpose of
our meeting. So, apparently feeling that she was wasting
her time, my friend went as suddenly as she came, and
I never saw her again. Another Witness called on me
instead. For the third time I started the beginners'
publication, *Let God be True*, for our lovely baby and
new home led me to look at this religion with new eyes,
and it seemed to set a seal on it all. I continued my

studies faithfully every week, and was convinced that this was God's will for me. But I was surprised to find that I still had no power to witness from door-to-door. I *believed*, but had no force behind my conviction.

Our new home had nothing but bare necessities; it would take some hard work to add the comforts we desired, which meant that when baby was off my hands sufficiently I would need to find work to help achieve this, even though the Organization frowned upon it. These were our leanest times financially, and I did so much need further Jehovah's Witness books. I had some already, but needed others, and had also to pay the subscription for the *Watchtower* and *Awake*. Although *Let God be True* (p. 215) reads, "Persons unable to donate toward the work, but who are interested, may have the literature free or upon such terms as they desire to receive it", this is simply not true. Only on the rarest occasions are odd copies of the *Watchtower* given to interested people at their doors; one needs a six months' or a year's subscription in order to join in the Sunday Watchtower meeting, for a start. Then there is the book needed for the Tuesday meeting. Later I had very different treatment from Christian people, who after my conversion showered me with genuine Christian love, and with bibles and so many books that I could not keep up with it all!

Since we were short of money, I asked if I might buy separate copies of the *Watchtower*; the distributor called every week, so that it wouldn't have inconvenienced anyone, but I had to have a subscription. It is true that if I had gone to a church I would have had to put something in the plate; since there are no collections at the Kingdom Hall, that made things square. So I paid, hoping that I could conceal what I was doing from my husband. Actually, when the books and *Watchtower* started coming, he accused me of theft! and he was justified, since money was given to me for my housekeeping, food and the like, not to spend in this underhanded way. But Witnesses are forewarned that they must expect "persecution", even in their homes! One is so schooled to expect this, and is ready with answers for it all, from Scripture and *Watchtower* reading that when others speak in protest, one cannot see that these protests arise out of love and concern for one. The Witness is convinced this is a satanic attack, and the more people try to make him see reason, the more he is convinced of the rightness of the Supreme Theocratic Organization.

The long dry summer of 1959 was extremely bad for sufferers from hay fever and asthma. I relied on the doctor and the kindness of the neighbours to pull me through this most difficult and trying time, during which the Witnesses' lack of sympathy was something to marvel at. Christ was loved because of His mercy and compassion to men by means of healing and words of comfort. His followers continue this today, but one will never find this in the Watchtower Organization. I was severely criticized for not attending the meetings and for dwelling on my ill health. I was not being obedient and should make the endeavour. My breakdown in health was a satanic attack which I should learn to overcome; it was merely a question of mind over matter, for asthma was a psychological illness—nothing more. Most hurtful of all was the comment that I suffered from this complaint because I thought too much of myself, and that I had these attacks in order to draw attention to myself. If I concentrated more upon the Watchtower Organization I wouldn't have attacks; they only came because I was too introverted. I could have wept at such cruel words—and such accusations were made against some who were in a far worse plight than I.

That particular attack lasted between five and six months; it was very bad and was fatiguing, and week by week I had to confess that I could not study. How I wished for something easier to read! In my exhaustion I would have been more than happy to sit back and listen to those lovely Bible stories in their simplicity. But Witnesses do not read their Bibles verse by verse and chapter by chapter, but only the isolated verses picked out in the Watchtower publications. Jehovah's Witness children miss so much—and, above all, cannot know about the true life of the Lord Jesus Christ.

As time went on, I was strong enough to carry out door-to-door work with a more mature "sister". Much as I had prayed for guidance on this matter, it seemed as though the spirit had drained out of me instead of in, and I stood at doors without resource, praying for people to be out. I did not feel able to offer anyone any "good news". Certainly I lacked something, and for me the Organization lacked something, but I knew not what. In Luke 21:14-15 we are told not to meditate on what we shall answer, for we shall be given a mouth and wisdom. But I was never given these things. One day we visited a block of flats; it was obviously a bad time to call, for the mothers were all dressed ready to collect their children from school, and very edgy at the thought of being late. I was anxious not to delay them unnecessarily and wanted to make appointments to suit them, but I was rebuked by my fellow worker, for the Kingdom Message comes first. "No," I said. "Their children come first. If they ran into the road, we should never forgive ourselves." "Jehovah will take care of that!" "They don't know that, nor would the children!" I was concerned over this lack of thought for other people's anxieties, but their attitude was that we might not get another opportunity to call. The appointment system is not at all successful, for during the waiting period they may have had second thoughts about receiving us.

Then we made our way to another flat and met a very charming lady, who told us in a rather bewildered way that a relative of hers had joined the Witnesses and that she had not seen him or heard from him since. All I could do was utter a feeble "sorry!" and make a hasty retreat. It wasn't pleasant to see the hurt look on her face. The Witnesses' answer would be that one finds fellowship with other believers, and that the people of the world are forgotten, and it is quite true that anyone joining them must reject family and friends unless they too are in the Society, for they are of "the world" and if they refuse to accept our message, we must shake the dust off our shoes and leave them to their fate.

13

Rulers of Darkness

> *This wisdom descended not from above, but is earthly, sensual, devilish. For where envying and strife is, there is confusion and every evil work. (James 3:15-16).*

The more I prayed for help and guidance in talking to others, the more the opportunities seemed to dry up, and I dried up with them. The more I prayed for peace at home, the more we seemed to have the most terrible quarrels. Whatever I prayed for, I received the opposite. As a believer I knew that sometimes there is a waiting period before the prayer is answered, but I never dreamt that one could receive such a peculiar and frustrating outcome. I seemed to see miracles in reverse effect, and instead of the good I received the bad, and sometimes within an hour or so. If this was a blessing on the chosen, I should hate to be on the receiving end of wrath! Job and I certainly had something in common, for Job 10:15-17 shows exactly how I felt and thought, and Job's words were applicable to my situation; "If I be wicked, woe unto me; and if I be righteous, yet will I not lift up my head. I am full of confusion; therefore see thou mine affliction; for it increaseth. Thou huntest me as a fierce lion: and again thou showest thyself marvellous upon me. Thou dost renew thy witnesses against me, and increase thy vexation toward me; thou dost bring fresh hosts against me." I was trying in all sincerity to influence my husband, though the Witnesses did not approve of this. One's family and friends will be eventually impressed by one's persistent zeal and labours, and themselves become Witnesses because of this. But this does not work out in practice. In some cases the Witnesses went to great lengths to persecute the non-believer. I had

68

been very carefully and systematically instructed in ways to answer my husband's questions. As they had predicted, he tried to sow seeds of doubt, but I had been so prepared that they could not penetrate the granite-like surface of my belief. But he earnestly tried to find a chink in my armour, to prise it open and release me from the captivity of this controversial religion. But whatever he did or said, he was wrong, we were right—and we had an answer for it all. He told me that Jehovah's Witnesses had a high rate of broken marriages, but I had been schooled on that point too; it was satanic propaganda! But why had I been so carefully forewarned, if there was not a skeleton rattling in the cupboard?

I was very conscious that this faith had prompted only hatred in my parents' home. I tried to assure him that this was exceptional, and I did genuinely believe this, for I had not yet learned that this hatred and arrogance is shown in Witness homes throughout the world. This comes from the books they read. I often asked who had written these books, but they are anonymous, and no one knows; one can find only the name of the publisher. Once when I was doing door-to-door work, a woman asked me why there was so much hatred for those outside the Society. She certainly did hit the nail on the head, but I told her that we loved the human race, and were warning all men of God's war upon His enemies at Armageddon; we were actually preaching hope to all the enslaved people in this devil-controlled universe. Who was I kidding? Her or myself? Weren't we really trying just to save our own skins? Then I called on a most kindly gentleman who patiently tried to explain that we were in fact run by Communism. He seemed to speak with authority, but I was just as adamant, for we had abjured our right to vote in elections, and in Australia our brethren preferred to pay fines rather than submit to world-power. Our brethren in Russia were persecuted terribly. No! we were not communistic; we paid no allegiance to men. We were also very proud of the fact that Jehovah's Witnesses did not support Trade Unions, which in most cases had Communist backing. We could not be good servants to one earthly master, as Paul urges, and then seek to undermine him through a union, even if we lost the extra advantages that unions can gain by means of arbitration and strikes.

The average Witness is not touched with Communism; but he is so subject to brain-washing that the most intelligent person can soon be reduced to a zombie-like existence, obediently accepting anything which is offered him in the name of Jehovah, so that it would be possible for Communist, or indeed almost any other teaching to be slipped in quite readily.

I had no reason to doubt the integrity of Witnesses as employees until in later years I met them in jobs I held, and also knew others who worked alongside them. Often they are work-shy, but in their enthusiasm for the "truth" they spent all day trying to indoctrinate others, and provoking unrest among a firm's staff. Those who encounter them often feel that they would like to "wring their necks" to get a bit of peace! I knew of one supervisor; she had been in control of a workroom with great success for years, but everything she had worked for, and the girls' happiness, was destroyed in a few weeks by one such person who came to the place. These things are true in offices and factories all over the country, where their chief aim seems to be to cause trouble. As far as I can remember this gentleman was one of the very few who seemed concerned for my welfare or warned me of the unseen dangers.

At about this time my husband was working with a Roman Catholic, and I felt that this man was undermining all my endeavours to lead him into the Witnesses, much to my annoyance. One day my husband walked in about a quarter of an hour after my weekly study. To come home at such a time was most unlike him; I had said, indeed, that even if I were dying he still wouldn't leave work! Obviously this matter was extremely important to him, but I just took it as an attack on my ways, and was glad that he had wasted his time. But the following week he walked in again just as the study was at a close. His timing was perfect, and before I had finished introducing my visitors, to my horror and embarrassment he ordered them out of the house. The more I tried to calm the situation, the more forceful he was. He was not joking, he was not prepared to argue or be reasonable; he was in command, and out they were told to go, and not to come again.

I could have wept. All my work and all my faith upset in this one moment—and he was throwing away his own chances of obtaining everlasting life! It was that Catholic who was behind this. Just like these Christians, I felt. They were the leaders of this evil world; doomed to destruction themselves and making certain that they took everyone else with them! Things like this convinced us that we were a Theocratic Organization. The Scriptures had promised us hatred and persecution in the last days, and even our relatives would betray us. "Ye shall be betrayed both by parents, and brethren, and kinsfolks, and friends; and some of you shall they cause to be put to death. And ye shall be hated of all men for my name's sake" (Luke 21:16-17). But Jesus had a word for these Catholics and their priests, capering in their long robes, "Beware of the scribes, which desire to walk in long robes" (Luke 20:46).

Yet even in my fury, I remembered that the Bible declares that the wife is under the subjection of her husband, and I realized that to love, honour and *obey* was being disregarded. Things settled down surprisingly well between my husband and me; for a time I felt physically and spiritually wounded and hurt; and yet (it occurred to me) if my husband did get converted to the Witnesses how would it affect us as a family? The result would be poverty; personal ambition and the sense of achievement would go, and he would hand himself over, lock stock and barrel to the Organization, which would cramp his personality and turn him into a Watchtower robot. I realized that I didn't want this life for him, and the prospect of our living together under the harsh Watchtower rules and regulations was as bleak as Dartmoor prison in winter, and just about as inviting.

I was rather surprised when the Witnesses came again the following week, as though nothing had happened.

I was particularly grieved by my husband's behaviour, because I had taken so much care not to disturb our way of life together; I had hoped to win him over by my way of living—"In all things shewing thyself a pattern of good works: in doctrine shewing uncorruptness, gravity, sincerity" (Titus 2:7). I felt that I had refrained from the awkward goings-on of some Witnesses, and I think that he had appreciated this; but he had apparently recognized the danger signal in some of the things I said. Besides this, my husband had met quite a number of Witnesses through his work, and had found them very unscrupulous. Other men had told him of the difficulties they were having with their wives once these people had visited them while the men were away at work; they didn't show up when the men were at home, which seemed underhanded. At the time I would not believe this; once again, as Scripture said, this was the "persecution" which must be expected. As I write this today, I realize how concerned my husband must have been; he had been on the receiving end of their hatred, and had seen for himself the effects on me during the months before we were married. He was determined that history should not repeat itself. I had believed that my experiences in my parents' home were out of the ordinary, but now I realize that I was but one among thousands to suffer in this way.

My husband realized that the Watchtower teachings were enveloping my whole personality, and strangling me in the process. It was all affecting my health again; I was feeling both physically and mentally ill. I could find no comfort or peace of mind at all. Many, many times I turned to God in prayer, but there seemed to be no answer. I was utterly depressed; my religion didn't help at all, I couldn't wait until Armageddon; I needed aid, comfort and guidance and above all understanding—but who could give it?

Through my personal sufferings I became fully aware that the Watchtower teaching was totally inadequate. There was nothing to lead me to a closer committal to the Society, for I lacked the inner conviction, comfort and satisfaction which I might pass on as I went from door to door. *I* was the lost sheep, standing on doorsteps and looking for a Shepherd!

14

Desolation

Having made known unto us the mystery of his will, according to his good pleasure which he hath purposed in himself. That in the dispensation of the fulness of times he might gather together in one all things in Christ. (Eph. 1:9-10).

Anyone else would have realized that I must come right away from the Witnesses, but I was too much enslaved for this, and I was determined for *us* to pass through Armageddon. All the same, I began to dread the arrival of the *Watchtower*, and when I saw a new issue poking through the letter-box I was apprehensive at the thought of Jehovah's fresh demands. I ought to have been going regularly to the Kingdom Hall, at least on Sunday evenings for the Watchtower Study, but this was difficult, for only on Sunday evening was my husband free from the building project he had been working on for the past two years—the only evening when we could have our meal comfortably. I knew that I must stay with him, and once the self-build housing scheme was completed (within six months, or perhaps a year) I would be free to work and study as I wished. If I did not look after his homecoming he would feel neglected, and would certainly not come into the truth. When it was all over I could then put my whole heart into the Society. But they didn't understand. One must attend; even in sickness there is no excuse.

The building project which my husband was engaged in was a "Self Build Scheme" where a number of men worked together to erect their own homes. This long and arduous task was helped by a bit of encouragement, but the Witnesses just sneered at it all. "What do you want to do that for? Armageddon is coming to knock it all down. What a waste of time, when you could be working for the Society!" But where were we to live in the meantime? They never gave a proper answer to that. They insisted that I had been "called" to do Jehovah's work of preaching the "Kingdom Message" from door-to-door, as Christ did, and I must follow in His footsteps. Family ties must come second; after all, Scripture showed that, in such passages as Luke 14:20. I could not contradict the Scriptures. But I had *not* been called by God to do this work; that much I did know. I had lived nine months in a convent and seen women who had answered the "call"; they seemed to possess an inexplicable aura. I had also met others who had a different call, to work in the outside world. I was conscious that I had not the right temperament for this work. Often when calling on church-goers it upset me that I was expected to strip them of their belief in the Trinity, Heaven and Hell, and other great matters, for I always had pleasure in meeting such people, and preferred to talk about the things we had in common, especially the beloved Scriptures, and really to have a heart-to-heart talk which we both enjoyed. This often got me into hot water with the other Witnesses, though.

From my convent days and for years afterwards I had set my heart on missionary work. True, my asthma was a handicap, but surely God would either heal me, or find me some work which I could do as I was. If it was not His will to heal me, train me and send me abroad, as I hoped, what would He do with me in this country? I had no special ability and no training; I was not brilliant. I had just myself to offer; what was the Lord going to do with that? I had been so certain that He would use me. But the Witnesses announcement that I had been "called" was too cold, harsh and impersonal; there was no driving force about it. I wanted my calling to be straight from God, without an earthly interpreter. Once again I fell into deep depression. Clearly, I was not one of the chosen few to work for Jehovah. He had chosen His elect—and I was not one. I was still very distressed, too, by my husband's reaction, by his deliberate rejection of salvation at Armageddon. This amounted to suicide. The prospect

74

of going all through Watchtower disciplines and through Armageddon just to save my own skin seemed pointless. Yet there was Luke 17:34, "I tell you, in that night there shall be two men in one bed; the one shall be taken, and the other left". That text was much used to emphasize how God will separate families and friends, and how we must recognize this. Actually, of course, that text and the following verse speak of two men and then two women, not of a man and his wife. But my husband had made his stand on the other side, which meant complete destruction, and there didn't seem much point in living; the meaning and purpose of life would be swallowed in everlasting death, for in this religion it was not a matter of trusting in the Lord; salvation rested upon whether or not people had embraced the Watchtower beliefs while they had the opportunity. It is then, and only then, that God makes His mark and writes the passover sign on one's forehead. There was no hope and no reprieve. If only I could talk to someone about it all! But that would be disloyal—and anyway no one would understand. They would probably laugh and advise me to finish with it all. But I couldn't finish with it; but it was too deeply ingrained; it had eaten its way into me, and carved itself upon my mind. I just had to live with it.

Suddenly I had a desire to spread my wings and to see the world which I missed as a teenager. Now that we were better off, I was able to have pocket money, so that I could take myself to a dance every week. This started off well enough, but I enjoyed the bright lights and music too much to be satisfied with a small dose, and it became more often, and then a film midweek as well. There wasn't anything wrong with these pleasures in themselves, of course, but more and more they became a drug which I couldn't live without. I just existed until the next outing, and the days I spent at home seemed long and boring. I was addicted in the full sense of the word, and husband, child, home and religion began to mean nothing to me any more. Here again my religion failed me, and I had nothing to combat this fever. But now I had less and less interest in the Watchtower Society, for whenever I was with them there seemed to be such huge problems to cope with, which only Armageddon could settle. I was longing for a personal call from God to my heart; this formal election did not answer my needs, and they were certainly not answered by the cold comfort of waiting until Armageddon.

For some time now my husband and I had been at odds. He was more violent and forceful, while I relied on the sharper instrument of the tongue. His actions were very much out of character, for generally he was kind and patient, and his outbursts could not be explained. It seemed as though some invisible force was controlling the situation. After a quarrel we would look at one another and ask what it had all been about. These things went on for a long time, and something had to be done. I fled with our son!

This was the greatest turning point in my life for without the responsibility of a husband's salvation in my hands I saw a clear picture of the witnesses at work. It was years later and living in much happier circumstances I often pondered over God working through my husband, for as odd as it may appear I was convinced it was God's plan that I should leave home for a while. But the battles, strife and anxiety, surely this couldn't be the work of God? But it was made clear when I read 1 Sam. 16:14. "But the Spirit of the Lord departed from Saul and an *evil spirit from the Lord* troubled him."

15

Busybodies

And withal they learn to be idle, wandering about from house to house; and not only idle, but tattlers also and busybodies, speaking things which they ought not. (1 Tim. 5:13).

Back in my parents' home, my passion for the bright lights subsided immediately. It was a wonderful relief to be free from so many conflicting loyalties, concerning husband, religion and God. I got a job in Brighton, and there was a ring of destiny in this, for my three colleagues there and I were surely meant to meet, each to learn the lessons of human compassion and understanding from the personal crises which we each had to learn to overcome, during the year we were together. But although things were easier in some ways, often I was depressed and full of self-pity. There was the prospect of divorce and the stigma attached to it. I recalled my husband's earlier apprehensions, which now seemed justified, though it was hard to see just how things had come to this. But I still had the dogmatic Watchtower attitude of always being right, and I dismissed the whole thing from my mind. But now three things happened in quick succession, and forced my eyes open, so that I discarded for ever the Watchtower spectacles, never to wear them again. This period was surely the turning-point of my life.

One particularly grey and miserable Saturday afternoon, coming from work with my heart in my shoes, I brooded on the people who committed suicide, and I could understand how they must have felt—a sinking down into the depths of despair beyond the help of anyone. How I sympathized with them! for I was in the same mental sphere. When I arrived home, I found that a Witness acquaintance of mine was waiting in the front room. *Why* had mother let her in? My despondency turned into anger, but I calmed down a bit when I saw the hurt look on mother's face. "Well, dear," she said, "you have been so quiet lately and not your usual self, shutting yourself up indoors when you're not at work. I've been worried about you, and I thought you ought to have a Christian to talk to who would understand; so when I saw her and she asked after you, I thought I'd invite her over!"

"Well," I said, "You got her here; now you get rid of her. I want my dinner!" We were both quite determined, but mother was bound to win, because she held my dinner as a bait! When I faced my former associate she nearly blasted me off the face of the earth with fury and rebuke, because I had left my husband. She did not wait for the facts; she showed neither love nor compassion; she hurled text after text at me instead and demanded that I return to him. She did everything she could to hurt and wound. There was much that was right in her basic position; my place was back at home, but her way of declaring this was cruel, not helpful. The Witnesses are well known for their intrusions at the crisis-times of family life, acting with a sadistic cruelty rather than with love and compassion. Such actions can only be described as sheer cruelty—and all in the name of God!

Certainly in my own case this attack sent me into the depths of despair, without hope or any glimmer of light. I could see how people get to the point of suicide. But something happened; it was not a vision, but a very vivid realization that if I took my own life I would be accountable to God for what I did. I seemed to be taken out of my body and set before the Lord, and He said to me, "Who are *you* to take the life *I* gave?" Immediately then I entered my body again. Such an experience was quite contrary to Watchtower teachings, for I had realized that I had a soul which could leave the body at death, whereas they maintain that at death the body disintegrates in the grave, to be resurrected *after* Armageddon, but that there is no soul to pass on to heaven or hell. *Let God be True* says (p. 287) "Those who died wicked, beyond reform or *correction* and beyond redemption by Christ's blood will not be brought forth from the grave to judgement in the New World" and (p. 288) "Those goatlike persons who show no appreciation of God's kingdom but who reject the Kingdom message and its bearers and who show them no help and kindness will be destroyed in the coming battle of Armageddon".

Since I had returned to my parents we had moved into Brighton, where no one knew us and we were accepted without question—parents, their daughter and daughter's child. Winter was approaching and the boy would soon need warmer clothes. I was still wondering what to do when our neighbour told my mother that *her* mother-in-law would like me to buy the material for a coat and matching trousers for him! So my biggest financial worry was solved quite unexpectedly by this anonymous friend, whom I never met. She was a Roman Catholic, I was told, with a gift for needlework, and counted it a privilege to use this gift to the Lord's glory by making clothes for children who needed them. It was wonderful kindness! Now which of these two women was the true follower of Christ? Surely the one who saw my need and answered it so speedily and kindly!

I had got to the point now when I wanted nothing to do with God or religion. I was beaten down and broken. I did not want to believe, but above all I wanted to escape guilt complexes. Until now I had longed that my family should be converted; but I knew that I did not want my darling little boy to be exposed to all that I had been through during the last ten years. As I watched his lovely chubby little face on the pillow, as he lay with closed eyes, the softness of his baby features, I vowed with every ounce of strength I had that I would save him from that. For the moment I wanted to be left in rest and peace of mind; I just couldn't take any more! I prayed about my boy, for I wanted him to be brought up to love and respect his Heavenly Father, and I decided that when he was old enough to understand these things I would seek guidance, and then we would worship together. But at present I was like Job—"Are not my days few? *Cease then, and let me alone,* that I may take comfort a little" (10:20).

16

Conflict

For God is not the author of confusion, but of peace. (1 Cor. 14:33).

After much thought I told my father all that I had gone through with the Witnesses. I asked him to keep this confidential and not to tell mother, but actually he broke my confidence, which was most unlike him. Only two or three days later a door-to-door worker called, and mother told her all this. But she said that as I was not a baptized member, their rules did not apply to me. I thought this entirely wrong, for baptized or not I still believed and needed to make my stand of faith and live accordingly. Within a day or so friends visited us; I retreated to my room rather than go through all that again, but of course they heard the story from mother, and they gave a different opinion. This, a third opinion was expressed—that if I was going to attain to everlasting life, I must free myself from the matrimonial web, which could only lead me to everlasting destruction. These Witnesses did, then, seek to separate me from this earthly life. They urged that since my husband was one of the devil's children, he, knowing that he was going to be destroyed at Armageddon, would do all in his power to pull me down with him. All this proved to me that the Witnesses do not always say the same things, as they claim; certainly the studies are the same throughout the country, indeed throughout the world (for all the material comes from the Watchtower headquarters in America). Yet on one human problem which does affect so many people, there were three conflicting points of view, offered well within a week! Yet *This Means Everlasting Life* says (p. 125).

God's organization is an orderly, well connected

arrangement of his devoted, obedient creatures in order for them to work together toward a common end and in harmony with his purpose, doing so in peace and oneness, without clash or conflict with efficiency and a comfortable state of heart and mind. God's organization is at one with itself. All its members are at one with its great Organizer, Jehovah God, and at one with their obedient fellow members. God's perfect wisdom made his holy universal organization that way.

17

Food for Thought

I have dreamed a dream, and my spirit was troubled to know the dream. (Daniel 2:3).

Soon after this I had to go to the dentist for a couple of extractions. While I was under gas I had a dream which really shook me and made me question my intention to free myself from the marriage bond. In this dream I was in a law court and was asked to give evidence against my husband. I was to tell everyone in the court about his transgressions. I refused, because it was terrible to expose the faults and frailities of an ordinary human being without a word on the other side. Counsel prompted me, but I refused again. Others in the court joined in, kindly but firmly. Then I shouted at the top of my voice "I can't! I can't!" I screamed as though I was trying to rend the heavens, and the faces leered... "Oh, come along, Mrs Tomsett! Mrs Tomsett! Mrs Tomsett!—it's all over now!" and I awoke, to find myself still sobbing, tears pouring down my face, but my crying turned to joy in sheer relief to find myself in the surgery, but of course I was rather embarrassed over my outburst.

"You certainly must have something on your mind to react like that!" said the dentist. I nodded in agreement and inwardly thanked him for his understanding.

This was a real blow to my confidence, for until then I had been quite confident that my intended course of action was right. I had thought that I was beyond any emotion; I was indifferent to love or hate, and incapable of such things! I had told myself that my husband was just another human being, whose existence need not make any further difference to me.

I smiled ruefully to myself at the thought of making such an awful scene in court! Dreams don't normally bother me, but this one did, and it haunted me for many weeks, because it was so factual and so coherent. Most dreams descend into stupidity, and if one remembers them at all on waking, they are good for a few laughs. But I was puzzled about this one. I could not understand why I had acted so, but there seemed to be some purpose and meaning in it. It pointed forward to something—but to what? and when?

18

Busybodies Again

But let none of you suffer as a murderer, or as a thief, or as an evildoer, or as a busybody in other men's matters. (1 Peter 4:15).

One evening later on, while two Witness friends of my mother's were in the house, my husband called. As usual, I had retreated to my bedroom. He wanted to see me, as he heard that I had been ill, but mother panicked. She was so anxious not to get involved in our disagreements, and she asked him to go away and not bother us. Her friends declared that he ought to be arrested for causing a breach of the peace, and that they would give evidence that he had only come to make trouble. In actual fact his coming and going were uneventful enough, and he left without much ado. I could hear voices, but only an odd word here and there, and lay in bed going hot and cold, knowing that I was the bone of contention, but having no intention of taking part in all this. I just went on reading as I lay there, and decided to tell him not to call again, for there was nothing to be gained and it was not fair to my parents to involve them in our differences. I did not intend to write to him, but thought that I would either tell him this when he collected the boy from me on Saturday (the day arranged for him to have access), or to send word through the solicitor.

Actually a few months before, a solicitor's letter had been sent to him, threatening him with court proceedings should he call at my parents' home again, though on that occasion he was merely bringing a letter which had been sent to me at his address. I listened to what they told me, but I decided that if I was called on to give evidence, I would testify against *them*. I agreed that he should not have called, but he had done no harm; and I felt that I must see justice done, even if this meant jeopardizing the divorce proceedings.

It amused me no end to think of Jehovah's Witnesses giving evidence against him, when they are such a continual nuisance, calling at people's homes with their propaganda, with a persistence which it needs strong-arm tactics to overcome! Anyway, the Witnesses refuse to take the oath on the Bible which is available in the courts, and this could lead the judge to impose a fine upon them for contempt of court—so that the whole scheme was fantastic. That was the last straw and final evidence as to the integrity of these people. Surely it was not a Christian action to go to law! 1 Corinthians, chapter 6 states clearly that one should suffer injustice rather than resort to law.

Soon after this my parents told me that I must go: I had only two days' warning of this. I was very surprised, and the only thing I could do was to return to my husband. This I did, but very apprehensively, and wondering if our troubles would all start again. We had gone on such different ways of late; could there possibly be happiness for us still, or were we totally incompatible?

I wondered what to do, but next day at work my husband telephoned me. I don't remember if he said "Hallo!"—it seems to me that he simply said, "When are you coming back home?" I have never known what prompted him to ring at so opportune a moment; I could only get out the one word "Tomorrow!"—and that was how it was. Here again I was faced with something not of my own choosing. There seemed to be an air of destiny about my life :; it seemed that I was being propelled by a mighty invisible power—leading me where? I wondered why I should receive such V.I.P. treatment from the powers above!

My colleagues at work were so excited and really rejoiced. I received wise counsel from them; how kind they were! So, dressed in my best bib and tucker, and with a new hair-do, I took a taxi home. My "welcome home" was fit for a queen—a lovely bouquet, beautifully got up in ribbon and cellophane, awaited me; the bungalow gleamed with polish, floors and furniture alike, and all my belongings (which had been delivered earlier in the day) had been carefully put away. The people I met during the following days treated me like the long-lost relative that I was! I had never dreamed that people could be so kind—a convincing answer to the Watchtower teachings that everyone who was not a Witness was evil! When the front door closed behind me I knew that all would be well. Our trials were over, and our time apart would help us to find the union which God had ordained.

It was obvious that we had learned much through our separation; home had a new meaning, and everything was different, though one couldn't explain it. What was in the future was immaterial; good and bad would pass, but the power of protection was there. Later on, when I had been converted, I began to see the meaning of all that had taken place in those years, and it is fitted closely together like a jig-saw puzzle.

I was so thankful that I had not been given the power to witness freely, so that I had not urged others into that way of life. At the very outset my husband had foretold that our marriage would break up if my association with the Watchtower Society continued. I hadn't believed him, and I would not believe either that other marriages had gone the same way. I thought that his enmity was just the usual "persecution" which Witnesses are promised, so that long before I even thought of leaving him we knew that things had gone wrong. Others who have been Jehovah's Witnesses have since assured me that the break-up of marriages is very common. The various reasons are:

1. The attitude of the unbelieving partner is taken as a personal rejection.
2. Witnesses are warned that the unbelieving partner will be ready to persecute at every opportunity.
3. Witnesses decry the bearing of children, and also the normal happinesses of the home.
4. Marriage and children are a hindrance to the Theocratic Organization and to the struggle to get through Armageddon, and therefore every-

thing that has to be done for the partner and the children is allowed only under sufferance.

5. Since they are taught systematically to rebel against all authority and to do as they please there is bound to be trouble.

6. There is no room for love of the partner. There is much unhappiness in homes where a Witness is joined to someone who does not believe. It is just a matter of living together, the essential tasks performed without love or care. The unbeliever is persecuted until he or she is at last so exhausted and brainwashed that such one gives in, just to get peace and quiet. Life under these conditions is absolute hell, with the Witness continually mocking the unbeliever, who is commonly referred to as "the goat".

7. The Watchtower Society becomes such a bone of contention that mere toleration is all that can be hoped for.

8. A Witness will feel free to go off with another Witness, each leaving the non-Witness husband or wife. Inevitably it is the non-Witness who suffers from this instance of the eternal triangle. But many Witnesses are extremely arrogant, and believe that they can live in adultery and still find themselves pleasing in God's sight despite Watchtower warnings on this matter.

9. Whilst in the Watchtower Society many have just tolerated the unbelieving partner, perhaps for years. But if disillusionment comes, and one finds oneself with no faith and a ruined life, it is very easy to feel that the only practical thing to do is to make a clean sweep of everything—to leave home and start again, instead of patiently looking to see what could be recovered.

10. When a person has been entirely engrossed in the Watchtower Society and then finds a flaw in it all, he can be left high and dry, but still with all the energies which he has been devoting to the cause. He feels at odds with everything, and to form an improper liaison with someone of the other sex gives him some satisfaction in this

mood. Such a person now needs much love and care, but who will give it? With a home in shreds he will find solace somewhere.

11. The Witnesses are very strong against a church or civil wedding ceremony and say that these are only man-made. They also inveighed against wedding rings, which, they declared, came from pagan Rome and had been adopted in Christendom. There was much concern about this, and Witnesses I knew decided to keep their rings because of their sentimental value. Many, though, preferred to obey the Society and to slight their unbelieving partner, and caused further marital trouble.

12. If, as they teach, the devil is the prince of this world, the home is part of his sphere. But although Jesus did speak of the prince of this world (John 12:31). He also said, "All power is given unto me in heaven and in earth" (Matt. 28:18).

Love is essential to the home, but this Organization has no place for love. For them marriage is based on sex, and they deny one's right to bring children into the world, though surely that is the main reason for marriage. One must turn away from relatives, too, for the sake of the Society. It was an amazing thing for me to *leave* a "Christian organization" in order to find love, when the Bible is brimming over with the words of Christ about this. In the light of the faith I now hold, I can see another reason for the hatred they showed in the months before my marriage. They did not know what love really is. "What on earth do you want to get married for?", was the usual sneer. "You must be mad!" I must confess that they made me feel uncomfortable and even embarrassed that I could not explain myself. But I would say, "I love him, I want to live with him, cook, keep house and have children. I want to live a decent, normal life, the same as other people." But they were too loveless to understand what real life is like. I remember that on one occasion I was going through this, and my temper got rather frayed through the continual argument, and in sheer desperation I shouted, "For Christ's sake, shut up!" But still they went on, "Why? Why?" "To make it legal!" I was so angry that I just said the first thing I thought of. They didn't say a word, and I thought that I had shocked them into temporary silence, but in my ignorance I had at last touched on something that they understood. I had in fact hit "their" nail on the head; for marriage only takes place on that ground in their circles.

19

Christn and the Church

I have loved you with an everlasting love; there-
fore I have continued my faithfulness to you.
(Jeremiah 31:3) (RSV).
For you were straying like sheep, but have now
returned to the Shepherd and Guardian of your
souls. (1 Peter 2:25) (RSV).

During the next three or four years I took little heed
of God, but lived like the heathen—"Let us eat and
drink; for tomorrow we shall die" (Isaiah 22:13), but
the beauties of nature brought the thought of the
Creator to my mind. When our son was old enough to
attend Sunday School and understand the things of
God, continually I seemed to be reminded of my last
prayers, years before, that we should both worship together.

About this time something occurred, which made me
think. Someone criticized Billy Graham; I didn't really
know who he was, but he fancied he was a preacher.
But to my surprise I found myself saying, "If he came
over from America and was the means of saving one
soul, then his journey would be well worth while". I
was amazed at the conviction and force with which I
spoke; it was not really a bit like me. I knew nothing of
Billy Graham; I couldn't have defined the word
"saved", and it is foreign to a Jehovah's Witness (or, I
should say at that stage of my thinking, an ex-
Witness). But as I spoke I was convicted by a power
beyond my own personality; I knew that it was God's
power, and I wanted to worship Him. So one Sunday
morning we set off to a nearby church. Not having set
foot in church for worship for about fourteen years, I
felt rather apprehensive, and clung to the hand of my
little son. He was giving me moral support, and not I

him! "And a little child shall lead them," wrote Isaiah (11:6). I was impressed by the service and by our warm welcome. I had no thought at that time about attending regularly: I was just feeling my feet. But about six months later, while I was washing up, I was overcome by an urgent desire to join a Bible Study group, and I could not get rid of this. A few days later I was outside the church, and there was a notice about a Bible Study Group. The matter seemed more and more urgent, and I attended church the following Sunday morning. When they gave out the notices I was sure that I would hear something more of it, and was really amazed when it was not announced. I had to stop myself calling out to ask about it, for I was very disappointed and puzzled. I decided that I would make enquiries as I went out, but then felt that it might seem impertinent, since I was not a regular attender. However, with this in my mind, I made a point of attending the evening service, and to my delight it was announced that a new Bible Study would start on the following Friday. My premonition had not failed, and I had a further sense of a strong driving force.

Months later I learned of the strange experiences of the woman who organized these studies. She had been looking for an organization to get her materials from, and finally decided on one of them. She sent away for the necessary study papers, having planned the Friday when she wanted to start, but no parcel arrived. Her sense of urgency grew to such an extent that she went to London to get what she wanted. Even then it seemed that everything was against her; she got her fingers painfully squashed in a door, and then the heavens opened with such a downpour of rain that she was soaked to the skin, and stood, like a drowned rat, with clothing soaked and creased in a beautiful modern office waiting for the papers—while by then the sun appeared and shone brilliantly outside! Her sense of urgency about these study papers coincided with my own, and it looks as though the day I was outside the church pondering over the noticeboard she was in fact in London. It was wonderful to realize that although at that time we were unknown to one another, we were destined to meet and to discover our common bond.

These study-papers were from an Evangelistic Association, and instead of being told what to believe, one opened the Bible and searched the Scriptures, and to my joy the words came alive and were relevant to the day-to-day problems of the twentieth-century person. They dealt with the problems of faith, the praise and rebuke of Paul to the early church, and their problems are still our problems today. The temptations which men had to overcome then, we face today. What a wonderful revelation by the Prince of Light! Now the scales fell from my eyes, and I could see the glory and salvation of Christ. My first reaction was to regret the time I had wasted since I left the Watchtower Society. Yet I knew that I could not have come to seek God via the church much sooner, for although I had left the Witnesses I was still full of wrong beliefs and false doctrines, so that I would have found many reasons to disagree with other Christians. Physically and mentally, too, I needed a rest, and in my case time was a great and wise healer. I had prayed for peace of mind, and God in His wonderful wisdom granted me that, and He said, "My presence shall go with thee, and I will give thee rest" (Ex. 33:14). Further, I needed to learn to love my family in the true sense, and to achieve a rebirth and insight on all aspects of life, for I was like one of those described in Ezekiel 37—mere dry bones. "Thus saith the Lord God unto these bones; 'Behold, I will cause breath to enter into you, and ye shall live'" (v. 5). So He had spoken in Ezekiel 36:23-26: "And I will sanctify my great name, which was profane among the heathen, which ye have profaned in the midst of them; and the heathen shall know that I am the Lord, saith the Lord God, when I shall be sanctified in you before their eyes ... For I will take you from among the heathen, and gather you out of all countries, and will bring you into your own land. Then will I sprinkle clean water upon you, and ye shall be clean: from all your filthiness, and from all your idols, will I cleanse you. A new heart also will I give you, and a new spirit will I put within you: and I will take away the stony heart out of your flesh, and I will give you a heart of flesh."

This seemed to be a personal message for me. One's heart is spiritually of granite, which only a rebirth could soften.

The first five studies were so relevant to an ex-Jehovah's Witness. In these studies we were given the title, e.g., "Members of Christ's Body", and the key text—Romans, chapter 12, and we each studied this and then answered five short questions. It was intriguing to find that none of us came up to the meetings with the same Scripture quotations or the same ideas; for as it was a *personal* study we all delved into different parts of the Bible to discover what they said on our theme. There were six to nine people concerned and it was amazing how we learned from each other, and throughout we were in harmony.

What a joy to "search the Scriptures" myself, and not just to be told! We were allotted a small room, and we threshed our Bible harvest with enthusiasm, until the caretaker threatened to throw us out! "Just a few minutes more!" we begged, but he was wise to be firm and send us on our way—after all, we had been there three hours! We were equally enthusiastic in our preparations for our meetings. I certainly burnt the midnight oil, and was still wide awake at two or three in the morning. On this treasure hunt one's mind was so stimulated that sleep was impossible. What riches I found! I now understood what it meant to trust Christ as Saviour. "For God so loved the world, that he gave his only begotten Son, that whosoever believeth in him should not perish, but have everlasting life. For God sent not his Son into the world to condemn the world; but that the world through him might be saved." Just those two verses shatter the Watchtower claim that the world is in Satan's possession.

"Wherefore he is able also to save them to the uttermost that come unto God by him, seeing he ever liveth to make intercession for them" (Hebrews 7:25). Not the Watchtower Organization making intercession and offering the means to salvation, but our Lord Jesus Christ. I had learned and believed these things in my

Sunday School days, but these simple true doctrines of Christ had disappeared in the Society's highly intellectualist jargon.

Now with the help of Scripture I was rejoicing in personal communion with God. This is how Christians live, seeking the Lord continually, asking for the infilling of the Holy Spirit. The Witnesses know nothing of this; they know nothing of the warmth that is present when one feels the presence of the Lord Jesus Christ when He fulfils His promise, "Where two or three are gathered together in my name, there am I in the midst of them". (Matthew 18:20). Although I had been searching the Scriptures in the matter of prayer, I had been finding it very difficult to realize as something personal; also my previous experiences had left me very sceptical, so that I was ready to leave prayer to other people. But this was not to be, for one Friday evening as I walked into the room for our study, the leader said to me, "Well, how much praying have you done this week?" I was very much taken aback and felt very embarrassed. I answered uncomfortably, "Not much!" which really meant "none at all". This was the second week she had challenged me in that way and I found it very uncomfortable. No one had ever spoken to me like that before; she must feel that the matter was important. However, she cheered me by saying that it would come, and it did!

I found myself talking to God in prayer. I found texts which encouraged me in this: "For the eyes of the Lord are upon the righteous, and his ears are open to their prayer" (1 Peter 3:12), and also, "Cast all your anxieties on him for he cares about you". (1 Peter 5:7). I began like a baby learning to talk; just a very few words, keeping it simple. Confidence grew with experience, and my prayers were being answered. I found this wonderful and was astounded by these promises of Christ's, that anything asked in His name would be given to us. I rejoiced that I had made contact with the Almighty, our Heavenly Father, and He with me, and so I could pour out my very being, knowing my words were heard. I had truly come to know that there is only one mediator between God and men—the man Christ

Jesus (1 Tim. 2:5). Worshipping Him in His church, I would know that solidarity which is so important for us if we are to keep strength, faith and fellowship. He was now alive, now a personal Saviour for me: I was no longer a cog in a massive earthly organization full of conflict and fear.

The Watchtower Societies condemn the churches for preaching "hell fire", but no church preaches this without also preaching the answer—the good news of One Who can save. It is difficult for the churches to oppose the Witnesses, for whatever they do they are accused of jealousy and (inevitably) "persecution", which the Witnesses take as a testimony to their truth. Whatever one does about them leaves difficulties. If we bury our heads in the sand and pretend that the Organization isn't there, or that it might go away, the more people seem to join it, or to be scattered like lost sheep through their persuasive and disturbing methods. Nothing is sacred to these ravenous wolves and their continual pillage.

The workings of the Society are so deep and complex that even the most skilful would find it hard to visualize what lay beneath its skin, let alone penetrate to its very heart. It would be a full time occupation to combat all its teachings, which change from day to day. William Schnell and Ted Dencher who, like Paul, were formerly zealous for this false religion, have given a full and true account. It is obvious that few people are aware of the extent of this powerful organization, which is world wide. It owns enormous printing presses, and has aeroplanes at its disposal, and its conventions are something to behold. Do not be misguided into thinking it is a "queer" religion for a few cranks; it is strong and powerful, and can make the churches appear very weak and insignificant. When a Witness sees thousands of people converge on some great centre every six months, it encourages them to believe that their way is right—and remember that 90% of that great concourse will be *active* Jehovah's Witnesses. (How many of the churches could boast that?) Truly does 2 Peter 2:2 say, "And many shall follow their pernicious ways; by reason of whom the way of truth shall be evil spoken of".

Reverting to their publishing programme, here are some figures:

The Truth Shall Make You Free	5,300,000	copies	1943
The Kingdom is at Hand	5,000,000	,,	1944
Let God be True	7,000,000	,,	1946
This Means Everlasting Life	2,750,000	,,	1950
What Has Religion done for Mankind?	1,000,000	,,	1951
From Paradise Lost to Paradise Regained	1,000,000	,,	1958

Over twenty-two million copies of six publications, in addition to the circulation of *Watchtower* and *Awake*! Within four days recently, Friday to Monday, in normal day-to-day encounters, I met or heard of eight Witnesses and former members. Eight in four days! One would certainly have to go out of one's way to find eight Christians just by chance!

A Christian believes that it is duty to take part in the government of his country; but by means of such texts as "We must obey God rather than man" (Acts 5:29), a Witness withdraws from any such concern. *Let God Be True* declares that the United Nations Organization was devised by the prince of this world and is in fact the beast mentioned in Revelation 17:3, 8, 11. "The beast that thou sawest was (the old League of Nations) and is not (being lifeless during World War II) and shall ascend out of the bottomless pit (as the United Nations Organization)". In other places this beast is equated with "organized religion". Revelation 17:6 reads, "I saw the woman drunken with the blood of the saints, and with the blood of the martyrs of Jesus; and when I saw her, I wondered with great admiration". But certainly persecution of this type is not known under the United Nations Organization! while under atheist dictator powers like Nazism and Communism such things are common.

I was unaware then of 1 Tim 2:1f, "I exhort therefore, that first of all, supplications, prayers, intercessions, and giving of thanks, be made for all men; For kings, and for all that are in authority; that we may lead a quiet and peaceable life in all godliness and honesty". If we opt out of the affairs of government, we leave the doors wide open for evil forces to rule and plunder. We have to live on until the Return of the Lord, and the Christian has a very important part to play in the world until then. But Witnesses refuse to accept that Parliament can influence the thinking of the people; but it is certain that if a Government's moral standards are high and founded in Christian principles, the moral standards of the people will be the same, and personal happiness increases. "When the righteous are in authority, the people rejoice; but when the wicked beareth rule, the people mourn" (Prov. 29:2).

When I began to learn continually great and new things from God's word in simplicity and truth, I was much concerned that I could not find my former associates who might still be enslaved by the Organization. Were they still in the darkness of prison, even if they did not know it? Even my parents had renounced me and refused to have any more to do with me after they thrust me out of their home in 1962.

Once a Witness ceases his door-to-door witnessing, although the Watchtower Society regards him as "lost" and eliminates him, he is really living in no-man's land and is still indoctrinated by the Watchtower teaching. Unless he is converted to the Lord Jesus Christ he has nothing to live by except the powerful influence of the Society which has dominated him for so long. This is the danger, because these teachings, remaining in the mind, create terrible psychological problems. For instance, a girl or boy brought up under Watchtower influences to believe that it is wrong to bring children into the world, may later leave the Society, get married and start a family. There may later prove to be a barrier between parents and children, attributable to this early training and influence. The life of such a person could be affected in a hundred and one ways by the early memories which linger on, and it may be that the more intellectual people are more subject to the influence of this highly intellectualist religion than people of a simpler kind.

But as for me, I was for ever comparing the old with the new, and breathing the sweet refreshing air of rebirth. I felt alive and thrilled, free, without fear. It was as though a door had been opened to greet a beautiful spring day after a particularly hard and gruelling winter.

Now I belonged . . .

20

Love

For God so loved the world, that he gave his only begotten Son, that whosoever believeth in him should not perish, but have everlasting life. (John 3:16).

Many would find it incredible that although I had been married for nine years I could not have given an account of the word "love". I had always worshipped my parents, but their love for me was changed over night by the new outlook which they drew from the Watchtower standards. I then lived under a rod of correction, rather than the love which came from the Lord Jesus Christ. I could never understand this change of heart toward me. As time passed, I appeared to be hard and cynical. I could not have shown any emotion to anyone of the opposite sex; it would have seemed strange, since the deep things of the heart were never revealed in family life. So it had only been with my head that I had loved, and thus had lost a deep inner joy and happiness.

I thought I had married in the deeper sense of love, but as with so many marriages in these days the foundations were wrong. So when I left my husband, I went without concern. There had been no deep bond between us, and the connection was purely superficial. I ought to have recognized and valued his devotion, which had been such a tower of strength to me. But I had been brain-washed for so long by the Witnesses, and I failed to see the truth about him. It would be impossible to depict all the results, and the continual wounding one of another, which results from this religion of the Jehovah's Witnesses.

At our Friday evening Bible Studies, the Rev. David Copestake began to tell us of his interest in drug addicts, which he had previously shown in Bradford. He asked if we would be interested in helping him, and this sounded wonderful; for I had learned so much about the risen Lord Jesus Christ, the Saviour of us all, that I was bursting to pass on the "good news". For various reasons this work did not last very long, but I learned so much from it; not mere theories, but the way of love in action, as inspired by the life and words of Jesus Christ.

Through Mr Copestake I met, or heard sermons by, such people as John McNicol, the late Rev. Mr Erswell, Janet Dryer and Frank Wilson, all so concerned in Christian love and caring, and twice went to Spelthorn St Mary's, a convent in Surrey, where a wonderful work is being done for those who are bound by drugs and alcohol. I saw tears of love and compassion shed over bodies broken and racked with pain through drug addiction. One girl, not twenty-one, was told that she had only two years to live. Only God knows the prayers, the tears—or the rejoicing—as she alternatively plunged into hell under the dominance of the drugs, or declared that she would have no more of them. At her worst, she would wave her syringe in my face and shout, "This is my god. Just you try and take it from me!" Through the degradation of these beatniks and drug addicts, I saw myself before my conversion. I was a bit cleaner on the outside, perhaps, but the inside (which is what really matters) was the same, the aimless, pointless living, the sitting around waiting (in my case until Armageddon). Some of these had that loveless background which leaves a purposeless vacuum into which one drifts, mentally and physically, so that nothing matters. Because of my past experiences, I knew that we spoke each other's language. I found myself believing in love and for the first time in about fifteen years or so, I felt the stirring of an emotion which I thought was dead, an emotion which leads one to understand so many of the secrets of God and man.

I also saw for myself what a mission is discharged by men and women like Mr Copestake and his friends, all in the love of the Lord Jesus Christ. My former brethren of the Jehovah's Witnesses decry all such activities as man-pleasing, and self-glorification. Such talk is only an excuse, to evade such tasks; yet I found quite a few of the youngsters caught up in this world of sleeping around, on the road, and of the junkies, had in fact been Jehovah's Witnesses, or their friends or parents were. It is not surprising that they should now be living in this way, for I myself was taught that I should become a social misfit, and not to conform to today's standards of living, to opt out and wait for Armageddon, because (they said) the so-called "respectable" way of living is inspired by Satan.

It is often claimed that drugs are illegally smuggled into this country and into America by Communists who want to cripple and demoralize western youth, and this could well be so, for their personality and intellect become indoctrinated by Communism. Youngsters who believe that they are supporting pacifism, etc., through their own volition, have sometimes been affected by drugs, which clear the way for systematic brainwashing.

I realize now what it was that caused my failures in career and in marriage; for I, who had formerly known the love of God, had accepted the Watchtower teachings, grounded in man's intellect and actions. These things cannot withstand life's challenge—but God's love is ours for ever.

21

Strength in Faith

He will bless them that fear the Lord, both small and great. (Psalm 115:13).

My faith increased and my steps were made stronger and firmer. I made new friends, and the doors of their homes opened to me, to reveal the Christian love and sincerity within. I was so ashamed of my former beliefs that I did not say a word about them, but this was a skeleton in my cupboard which gave me no peace until I did tell them about it. Their reaction was so different from what I imagined; I had feared that they would be horrified and shocked, but they were sincerely grateful for the Lord's divine mercy upon me. They had reason to know what mischief the Witnesses can do by infiltration into the families belonging to the church. One of the clergy did ask why some who had been of his church, who had sat in complete silence in their pews for years, were filled with courage and conviction the moment they joined this sect, carrying out door-to-door work with such zeal, their former quietness and inactivity completely transformed into high-pressure advocacy of Watchtower beliefs, and in next to no time giving addresses in the Kingdom Hall! Why couldn't they have witnessed for the Church in this way? The Church could do with such people! There is no doubt that a Jehovah's Witness can and does reproach most ordinary church members for their ignorance of the Gospel message and of the Bible, and also for their lethargy in outreach, especially in door-to-door advocacy of their faith. As the churches withdraw from this particular field they leave the Witnesses a clear run, and the Witnesses profit by this. When I worked for the Witnesses, I used to ask people, "When did you last have a visit from your church?" They would raise their eyebrows and shrug their shoulders and mostly say, "Never!", or laugh and say "Once in twenty-five years!", or "They only call when they're holding a jumble sale, or collecting for something!" As Jehovah's Witnesses we got into people's houses on the strength of this, only too pleased to have another reason to pull the church to pieces. The very fact that we were the only religious denomination to do work of this kind proved that we were God's chosen people! The churches would fail, we declared, because of this. "The Church couldn't care less about you, and this lack of visiting proves it, doesn't it?" This question always got them, and we had succeeded in harming the Church. Whether these people joined the Society or not, they certainly would not join in with church activities after that.

Further, many churches lack mid-week activities to train the Christian in his faith. Where there is only Sunday worship there is spiritual desolation mid-week, and this can lead to a falling away or a move to some place which fills this need. Finally, how many church members can boast that the Lord has blessed their church with His presence? Alas! many churches are only the scene of social activities, with the added *cachet* of the name "Church" written over the door. Jehovah's Witnesses can and do point to such places, and it is well known that the members of such churches do in fact wait for them to call to discuss the scriptures, knowing sadly that their own clergy and fellow church-members would smile at their concern. For many so-called Christians, Bible readings were long ago discarded as "old hat". However, there is no call for the Watch-tower Society to judge the churches. Christ Himself bestows praise *and* reproof in Revelation, chapters 2 and 3. The Church, after all, is people, not a building. So therefore when a Witness criticizes your church, he is criticizing you. If he does, go prayerfully to those Revelation passages, or others, and with Christ's help right what is wrong.

After a time changing circumstances led me to look for another church, which would continue to build me up in the new life. I realized the need for a lot of thought and enquiry. So I wrote to an Evangelical Association in London, telling them of my spiritual needs and asking which local church they considered most suitable to fulfil these. I didn't have to wait long for the reply, which named the church in Hove which people had been recommending to me. A few weeks later, I met a Christian lady "by chance", and after discussing our common interests, we gave each other our names, addresses and telephone numbers so that we could continue our talk later on in the comfort of our homes. It must have been a fortnight later when I made the first move and telephoned her, and during the conversation I mentioned my concern to find another church, because I needed a good strong powerful place, full of Bible—and prayer-meetings—and which would respect my belief in believer's baptism. She immediately said, "Come to my church!"—and it was the church which had twice before been recommended to me! This was surely a wonderful example of leading, testing and follow-up, between my conversion and my baptism. Unknown to me there were Christian friends praying for me. There were times when I could actually feel a spiritual uplift and had a sense of invisible protection. Later on, when they told me of their prayers on my behalf, I was able to tell them when they had been praying! During this period I had two very painful dental abscesses. One tooth was extracted but the second had to remain, for fear of the poison leaking into the lower cavity. Those months were physical hell, but through this I felt a drawing near and a closeness to the Saviour, and so felt His comfort and power with me.

Once when the pain seemed quite unbearable, and I had carelessly run out of the prescribed, extra strong, pain-killers, in sheer desperation I telephoned some of my Christian friends for their prayers. I really felt terrible, but a miracle did take place, for within twenty minutes not only was the pain eased, but I was in a most restful sleep. At the time of the extraction a very nasty abscess was revealed, and the dentist was much surprised at the small amount of discomfort it all gave me.

There was another instance which showed how prayer can over-rule difficulties. Just a few days before my baptism, I suddenly felt apprehensive; and although I had waited patiently for five months to honour our Lord's command I wanted to reject the whole thing. For two hours I battled against this idea that perhaps I was taking religion too far. Every possible argument against obeying this command of Christ's rose before my mind, and then these thoughts left me as suddenly as they had come, and I felt strong, confident, with a sense of exultation which lasted right over the period of the service.

When I went into church that Sunday evening, some of the women told me that I had been fully remembered in prayer. One such time of prayer had been at eleven o'clock on the previous Thursday, the very morning and the very time when my doubts fell away! These were only two instances of the power of prayer, and to me, an ex-Jehovah's Witness, who for years had prayed with no response, or who had sometimes seemed to be cursed rather than blessed, this was wonderful. I could hardly believe that the Lord Jesus Christ cared for me, and I rejoiced in this *belonging* to Christ, this realization of Matthew 28:20, "Lo, I am with you alway, even unto the end of the world": I knew the truth of 1 Peter 5:7, "Casting all your cares upon him; for he careth for you". The wonder of it all!—it seemed inexplicable. Sometimes the Lord in His wisdom sees fit to delay His answer to our prayers, and this, as every Christian appreciates, calls for patience. We need faith to understand that our Heavenly Father in His infinite wisdom answers prayer at the right time.

One day, I remember, I was very disappointed because a special prayer had not been answered. At the first opportunity I went into my bedroom, shut the door, and, sitting quietly on the bed, poured out my trouble to the Lord. I hadn't got very far when it seemed as though another presence was with me, bidding me read Luke 18. I tried hard to get into the spirit of prayer, but the bidding became stronger: *Luke 18 . . . Luke 18 . . . Luke 18 . . .* I felt rather disgruntled about this, but opened my Bible and looked at that chapter; my disappointment turned to joy and to confidence that my prayers were being heard, and that in due time, after yet more prayer, they would be fulfilled. More recently I had a rather difficult interview which I was not looking forward to, and really prayed hard about this. I experienced the same sort of interruption; this time the scripture was 2 Cor. 6:7, and I was encouraged when I read, "By the word of truth, by the power of God, by the armour of righteousness on the right hand and on the left". The Scriptures were truly unfolding themselves through prayer. I was unlearned in the Scriptures, and no one could attribute these messages to my own knowledge; this was revelation.

Another instance of great blessing came three years ago when our little daughter was born. Throughout my pregnancy I laid the whole matter before the Lord, committing us both to His safe keeping. After the birth of my son I had vowed that I could not face the ordeal again, and this fear had been with me through four or five years; but the dread had gone. On the rare occasions when I felt apprehensive my immediate reaction was to turn to the Lord, who comforted me with His love and care, and I looked forward to the birth with great joy. I can sincerely praise the Lord for that blessed, wonderful day in July when our daughter was born. This was a wonderful contrast to the time when my son was born, for that was under the shadow of the Watchtower Society, and without the upholding of the Father. That had given me the fear that every time of childbirth would be the same, but my second confinement, within the true Christian faith, was perfect. I didn't have to wait until Armageddon to achieve this!

22

Witnessing to the Witnesses

> *If any of you lack wisdom, let him ask of God,*
> *that giveth to all men liberally, and upbraideth*
> *not; and it shall be given him. (James 1:5).*

Since my conversion I have been very conscious of the
Lord's mercy in not only bringing me out of the Watchtower slavery but in leading me to Himself. Through
wonderful grace and salvation I can now worship in
complete freedom. But I am very conscious that many
thousands of people are still enslaved, and that daily
more are being drawn into the Watchtower Society and
so losing their opportunity of looking upon the Lord
Jesus Christ as Lord and Saviour. They are looking to
Armageddon for salvation instead—salvation in the
future, when they might turn now to Jesus as Lord and
Master and do His will, instead of obeying all the
demands uttered in the name of Jehovah, by the Watchtower Society. When an unbeliever or a Jehovah's
Witness turns to Christ the change is amazing—to realize that Christ is a personal Lord and that prayer is
personal too, with the sense of belonging to Him and
of His caring for you. The revelation is so tremendous
that it is difficult to put it into words. The unbeliever
rejoices when he finds Jesus, but the ex-Jehovah's Witness rejoices even more; for he has been blinded by his
religion and now is freed. He has been working and
praying to Jehovah, all to no avail. His prayers have
remained unanswered, and it has been like praying into
thin air; Armageddon has been his only hope. He has
been led to believe that *all* church people are under
satanic influence, which impels them to commit crime
and indecency; that they incite others to homosexuality
and perversion. The Watchtower Society does really
persuade its members to believe all this; they apply

every condemnatory word in the Bible to the clergy of today, and systematically thousands of Jehovah's Witnesses call upon people every day of the week to tell them all this. They approach gullible men and women who believe that they come from a Christian organization, and they are able to persuade the unbeliever; the backslider can be influenced, and many nominal Christians, particularly those with a grouse against their church, are easily drawn into the Kingdom Hall because of this. Admittedly, some ministers do hold heretical views, but the Watchtower teaching exaggerates all this so that according to them all Christians think and talk in this way. They even declare that the Church is the "beast" that is spoken of in Revelation 13:18.

A Christian should at all times remember that these people are enslaved by Watchtower thinking, and act entirely upon Watchtower commands, and that it is his duty to free them from this bondage, and lead them into the freedom of Christ. Yet when I was a Witness I found that few Christians were able to express their faith in Christ as a personal Saviour. During my ten years in the Organization I failed to find a single Christian who could do this. The most they would say was that they belonged to a church already, and were quite satisfied, "Thank you very much". Whatever spiritual troubles the Witness may know, he keeps going by sheer grit and determination, and the door-to-door work gives him strength and the conviction that even though his personal life may be difficult, the Watchtower Society has more to offer Christians than they can offer him. They seem so apathetic and unsure of themselves, to wave in the wind like reeds, with no concrete faith; and this seemes to confirm the Watchtower opinion of the Church. The attitude of the Christians as we visited door-to-door confirmed the importance of our work, for we were obviously the only religious organization seeking to spread the Kingdom message as Christ had commanded.

There are three reasons why a Christian should witness to the Jehovah's Witnesses when he has the chance:

1. They need a personal Saviour. Many, many scrip-

tures, of course, point to this; but they are taught that Armageddon is their salvation.

2. They oppose the church, and are a continual stumbling-block to some outside the Church who are seeking a true and satisfactory faith, so that homes are broken up; many have entered mental hospitals with nervous breakdowns.

3. They take the Scriptures out of their context, and you can even find half of one text being joined up with half of another from some other part of the Bible—which completely disrupts the whole meaning.

How many Christians think that the Lord might well be calling upon them to witness for Him when the Jehovah's Witness calls? Surely *these* are the lost sheep looking for the Shepherd, and you may very well lead them to Him. Born-again Christians ought to bear this in mind. Unfortunately they always seem to call at the wrong time—especially when the poor housewife is in the middle of cooking a meal, or has answered the door with hands covered with soap-suds or flour! This doesn't make one feel inclined to discuss deep matters of faith, especially if a burning smell comes wafting through! The best thing is to make sure that water and gas taps are turned off, and that all is safe in the kitchen, and then to let them give their well-rehearsed party piece, and get it all off their chest; they have rehearsed hard enough, and they will feel all the better for it! Then if that particular time is not convenient, make an appointment with them—and in the meantime pray that you may be guided to say the right thing when they come. The results can be astonishing. Prayer-partners are a great asset in this work, and if such partners can be "covering" when the discussion is imminent and when it is going forward, then this is marvellous. It is important to remember that their witness *is powerful*, and you must ask yourself if you really can tackle them. They are out to break down your faith and leave you with doubts and fears. Many people who tried to argue with them have ended up as converted Jehovah's Witnesses in the Kingdom Hall. You will be quite justified in refusing to talk to these people and in shutting the door politely and firmly in their faces. But you can pray for them, that some other Christian may be the means of bringing them to the Lord, for they are in great spiritual need.

However, if you do feel equal to the task, answer their set doctrine with the message of a personal Saviour, and of salvation *now*, not at Armageddon. You will be fulfilling James 5:20—"He which converteth the sinner from the error of his way shall save a soul from death, and shall hide a multitude of sins", and likewise Luke 15:7: "I say unto you, that likewise joy shall be in heaven over one sinner that repenteth, more than over ninety and nine just persons, which need no repentance."

If you do argue from the Scriptures, remember that some have their own translation of Scripture, so that they may argue about this. Also they have a book called *Make Sure of All Things* which urges that some texts are spurious, or which adds a word here and there, and thereby suggests that your translation is not accurate.

Remember too that they are well practised by means of speech training through their Theological School: they will approach you in a psychological manner. They are cool, calm and well-prepared, and can easily discourse for a couple of hours on subjects like the Trinity, the Deity of Christ, the Holy Spirit, the soul, Heaven, Hell, the Sabbath, Christmas, Easter or the crucifix. On and on the argument goes, without any real progress, until you become completely exhausted, and finally the Witness sails down the garden path, hale and hearty! You realize then how carefully he has edged the conversation round to *his* pet subjects, so that you lost the advantage within the first few minutes.

This happens to nearly everyone who tries to tackle these people, but in our weakness we find strength, and by that first encounter one is prepared for the second. I well remember, as a new Christian convert, zealously witnessing to a Jehovah's Witness who got the upper hand at everything I said. I was floored, and when we parted I felt so completely deflated. I was filled with shame at being so poor a witness for Christ; but from that experience I learned humility, and learned to lean on Him even more in situations of this nature. What amazes me is the fact that Witnesses of long standing (some are of the fourth generation) are still repeating *verbatim* the same old parrot-cry of Armageddon. They have in the past prophesied all sorts of things which have not happened, and *still* they cling to this doctrine. I can remember over a quarter of a century, when these people were calling on my mother, preaching the destruction of the world as something which was *then* just around the corner! Dates in the Watchtower publications have to be altered from time to time, to save their faces. When I married in 1957, it was much to their disapproval, for we wouldn't be here after 1960, so why get married for so short a time? Then there was the time when the Society built mansions for the return of Moses and Elijah—these are now being used by their V.I.P's!

Armageddon is nothing new to any Bible reader, but clearly the Watchtower have taken it upon themselves to be above Christ in knowing about His return; for they state that He is "come", and that He established His temple in 1914. This is precisely what the Lord warned us about: "Then if any man shall say unto you, 'Lo, here is Christ, or there', believe it not" (Matt. 24:23). They are doing just that. They believe and preach Armageddon, and anticipate being upon the earth at that time, but we read so clearly in 1 Thess. 4:17, "Then we which are alive and remain shall be caught up together with them in the clouds, to meet the Lord in the air: and so shall we be ever with the Lord."

As one attempts to bring the Gospel to a Jehovah's Witness, it must be done with love and compassion. Remember that we have been saved by the mercy of the Lord Jesus Christ, as we read in Ephesians 2:8-9, "For by grace are ye saved through faith; and that not of yourselves: it is the gift of God. Not of works, lest any man should boast." In thanksgiving we should make every attempt to pull another out of this fiery damnation. We read the parable of the Good Samaritan (Luke 10:30-37), about the man who was travelling from Jerusalem to Jericho and fell among thieves, who stripped him of his clothes and departed, leaving him half dead. This is exactly what the Watchtower Society has done to the Jehovah's Witnesses—stripped them of all their brain-power and intelligence. They are being battered and bruised by the continual Watchtower demands, so that they cannot see straight or talk intelligently; they are utterly broken down by this Organization, which has completely robbed them of all their spiritual belongings. So we as Christians should show mercy on them in the Lord's name, bind up their wounds, for they have many psychological ones; feed and nourish them with the unadulterated Word of God, and lead them to a sanctuary for rest and shelter.

Always refuse to discuss their books with them. We read in Gal. 1:8 "But though we, or an angel from heaven, preach any other gospel to you than that which we have preached unto you, let him be accursed". They will deny that they are using these books as another gospel, and say that they are Bible aids; but they *are* used in place of the Scriptures. It is the Scriptures which are used as additional to the books, and not the other way round, as they would suggest.

Nor should the Christian enter into an argument about other churches, for they will use this to attack *your* denomination, and condemn it. We are told clearly in Scripture not to judge another (Matt. 7:1-6, Rom. 2:1 and 14:13). The most important thing on these occasions is to witness your belief in the Lord Jesus Christ as personal Saviour, your personal testimony of how the Lord has changed your life since your conversion. More than likely they will tear down the garden path, screaming for an ambulance for you, declaring that you are mad or devil-possessed! But if every Christian did this, in the end they would have to listen.

Give them a testimony about prayer, too, for they do not know about answers to prayer. If enough Christians testified that the Lord does answer prayer, and perform miracles, as He did when He was on earth, and that He leads people to work for Him without tyranny of the Society, they would eventually have to take notice. Tell them what the Lord requires of you in service to Him, and say that in your own small way you are being used. All this is very important, for they are convinced that only the Society can give directions, and that the Lord does not call individuals.

Offer them the love of God, in place of the fear of Him. They are convinced that the fear of God is all-important, and so dismiss texts like John 3:16 and 1 John 4. In my time, I have had the fear of God rammed down by throat, and this leads to such frustration and inhibitions that eventually one turns from Him. Accept any literature that they may give you; do not buy any. Then read it prayerfully, mark it, correct it and give it back to them and discuss your readings with them, and offer them helpful Gospel tracts. Share with them a reading from the Gospel or some favourite text, asking them what this means to them personally, what they do not understand about it, and what impresses them most—and keep them to the subject. This must be done with the love, compassion and patience that Christ showed you before you were converted, taking the whole matter slowly and surely, as a mother would a child, as a teacher would a pupil. When they call, find out where they live and call on them, for the Lord says, "If a man asks you to walk one mile go with him two": call on them three times, and if their hearts are still hardened, bid them goodbye, as advised in Titus 3:10, "A man that is a heretic after the first and second admonition reject". If he still holds to the Watchtower Society instead of the unadulterated gospel of the Lord Jesus Christ, you will have to leave him, but you will do so with a clear conscience. Remember that Jehovah's Witnesses really do believe that faithful Bible interpretation can come only from their organization, so they will approach you with great patronage. Yet these people, who teach their members that the Christians fall back on the clergy for help with difficult parts of the Bible, do in fact draw all their teaching from the International Bible Students Association, otherwise known as the Watchtower Society.

The Witnesses attack the Roman Catholics for beautifying their churches with images and idols, which are at any rate a reminder of Christ's birth, His ministry on earth and His crucifixion, which was the gateway to our salvation. Their aim is to lead the Roman Catholic (or any other kind of Christian) to worship in a fashion which gives no revelation of Christ, the Son of God, Lord and Saviour, in the way the Christian worships Him.

A Christian would do well to approach the Witnesses in the faith of the Lord Jesus Christ. He could be the means of freeing them from their slavery and of realizing the promise that the Word of the Lord shall not return void. (Is. 55:11).

23

Surprise Letter

> *But there is a spirit in man; and the inspiration of the Almighty giveth them understanding. (Job 32:8).*

I neither saw nor heard anything more of the Jehovah's Witnesses for quite a while, and then I received a letter which disturbed me. My friends and I were full of praise and thanksgiving to the Lord for His many blessings, but obviously the religion of the writer did not satisfy her. I noticed once again the sense of promise in the future, not the salvation that we can know *today*.

Dear Householder,

I expect you are wondering just who is writing this letter. As a matter of fact I am one of Jehovah's Witnesses. When we were calling in your area you were not home, so I thought I would write.

As Bible students we meet many people who ask why God allows wickedness to continue. Have you ever wondered that? Also, many people wonder why it is that the wicked seem to get away with it all the time. It seems time to say that God-fearing people for the most part seem to get all the trouble. Do you agree?

The Bible shows that there is one person, super-human, who is responsible for all wickedness and suffering. I expect you have heard the expression "the Devil looks after his own". Well, it seems to be true. He tries to turn all mankind away from God. He doesn't have to try with the ones who are already wicked. So he does his best with those who believe in God. However, God promises an end to this wicked one very shortly, in the book of Psalms, number thirty-seven, verse ten and eleven. Then there will be complete peace on earth.

I would like to call to find out your own views on the subject.

Yours sincerely,
Mrs S. Atkinson.

When I answered her, I prayed that somewhere in my letter there might be some food for thought!

Dear Mrs Atkinson,

I read with interest your letter received last Monday though I don't entirely agree with your statement: "The Devil Looking After His own." He cannot fulfil complete happiness in his subjects as our Heavenly Father and Christ can do for us. We have only to meet a true Christian, feel and see the wonderful radiation that comes from him. Some of course have to face hardships, crisis and illness that befalls every one in time, but generally these trials and tribulations are a great witness to others, of the Glory of Christ to enable them to face these troubles with cheerfulness and grace which make the non-christians turn their heads and wonder what "they" had to give them such courage. Christ refers to himself as to the Light of the World, which I believe to be the greatest text in the Bible (personally speaking of course). Incidentally, this text was given to me at my own Baptism last year. John 8:12 refers.

We read in our daily papers, see on TV of the mass Drug Addiction that is seizing hold of our youth whose morals are at their lowest ebb, sex crime and all manner of corruption is in their hands. They worship these things and subconsciously they are Devil worshippers for only the Devil can provide all this filth freely. Our hospitals are full up with people suffering from nervous breakdowns and their main cause is lack of Christianity. In our Bible we read of Judas who was of the Devil who committed suicide and of the Gerasene Demoniac who was "demented" through evil spirits. With the above in mind, I don't believe that the Devil and his lot have much to offer.

117

You also state that it seems time to say that God fearing people, for the most part, seem to get all the trouble. Did I agree? No! Of course we all realize that temptations will come at our weakest moments as with Christ after His Baptism when He was hungry and weak with fasting but through this we have our re-assurance in: Hebrews 2:18 For in that he himself hath suffered being tempted, he is able to succour them that are tempted.

2 Thess. 3:3 But the Lord is faithful who shall stablish you, and keep you from evil.

Matthew 28:20 And, lo I am with you alway, even unto the end of the world.

By "trouble" you may have meant persecution which all through the ages we have had, Christian Martyrs who have undergone terrible persecution but have deemed it a great and wonderful privilege that God had chosen them to represent Him in faith even to death. In recent months I had the honour of listening to a Pastor who spent fourteen years in communist imprisonment. He had undergone so much torture, brainwashing, etc. that the American Senate (I hope I have the right department) declared that it was a miracle that he is living. Admitted that physically he is very sick and one can see at a glance that he is suffering now through those terrible ordeals, but the wonderful "glow and radiation" that shone from him as he spoke was indescribable. Far from being sorry for himself he realized that all was an Act of God and gave great glory to Him through his testimony. This was proof enough that try as the Devil might he could not take this man's life away. (How truly Matthew 10, from verse 16 rang in my ears). Even so, here was a most wonderful witness from our Lord, His love and faith that come what may He is our comfort and guide even in the depths of hell where I am sure that man must have been during these years whilst being ravaged by his persecutors. He also came out loving those who had persecuted him and praying for them as Christ commanded.

You also mention the Devil being responsible for

all the evil in the world, although we must not shut our eyes to this, but on the other hand as individuals we must praise God for the great and wonderful blessings we have been given to us daily by our Heavenly Father and our Lord Jesus Christ and with protection of the Holy Spirit as promised in John 14:26. Verse 27 goes on to say Let not your heart be troubled, neither let it be afraid. James 4:7-8 Submit yourselves therefore to God. Resist the devil and he will flee from you. 1 Peter 5:7 Casting all your care upon Him, for He careth for you. Psalm 62:8, Psalm 119:41-43 and Luke 18:1 are further texts which testify God's love towards us.

Of course most Christians realize the prophecies are being fulfilled and we are on the road to Armageddon and the Second Coming of our Lord, but we still have to live until that time as it would be most presumptous of anyone to predict this as we read in Matthew 24-36 "But of that day and hour knoweth no man, no, not the angels but my Father only". Also 25:13 Watch therefore, for ye know neither the day nor the hour wherein the Son of Man cometh.

In the Bible we read continually of the importance of prayer—Jesus prayed at nights. Acts 1:13-14 "devoted themselves to prayer". We are told in Luke 21:36 Always to pray and pray without ceasing. 1 Timothy 2:8 I will therefore that men pray everywhere lifting up holy hands without wrath and doubting.

In your little notelet which you also left I read that you recommend a book that has helped you to understand these things from the Bible but surely one goes to the Author, God Himself, for wisdom on this subject. Only He can interpret through the Holy Spirit. We pray for wisdom as we read in James 1:5. "If any of you lack wisdom, let him ask of God that giveth to all men liberally and upbraideth not; and it shall be given him. We read of Solomon praying to God for wisdom—which was blessed by God. There is also the prayer of Moses in Psalm 90:12, and Paul's prayers in Ephesians 1:16. Also Paul writing to the Colossians 1:9 prayed to God directly and was not sidetracked to other means.

I think I have covered your comments in your letter.

Yours sincerely
Valerie Tomsett

Her reply was full of Watchtower jargon and of claims that they alone were the Theocratic Organization, the chosen people of Jehovah. As I read her letter I could feel the Watchtower hardness, that invisible icy barrier, and I tore it into shreds and threw it away.

24

The Watchtower Society
and Children

But Jesus called them unto him, and said, Suffer the little children to come unto me, and forbid them not; for of such is the kingdom of God. (Luke 18:16).

Children are not encouraged to be born into this wicked world in which the Watchtower Society has placed in the devil's hands. They support this belief of theirs by Matt. 24:19, "And woe unto them that are with child, and to them that give suck in those days!" For Witnesses to become parents hinders the work of the Society, and further with children to care for one may not be able to stand up to the pressures of satanic attack, and thus one's chance of coming through Armageddon might be smaller. They consider the desire for children to be a carnal sin. Many proud parents-to-be have been rebuffed by a Witness, who will probably respond in a very abrupt way when told about the forthcoming event. The Society does not hold Baptismal or Dedication Services as the Church does, and they regard the children as of no consequence to anyone—least of all God. Some Witness parents do, however, secretly give birthday presents to their children. The children do not demur at the ban on gifts and seem to think that other children are selfish to expect such things. After all, they will be receiving the greatest gift of all, everlasting life, after Armageddon. Christmas Day is also just another day, but the Witnesses take advantage of the holiday to carry out as much door-to-door work as possible; whilst the "heathen" are "in the spirit" they can sell many of their publications. If anyone criticizes them for using Christmas Day like this, the Witnesses accuse them of making it an excuse for not joining the Society, and say "Fancy letting one day a year stand in the way of gaining everlasting life!" —a ridiculous comment, for the Christian gladly gives up fifty-two Sundays a year to worship the Lord, so if they were convinced of the "truth" they would also offer up to seventy Christmas days as well, in the course of a person's lifespan!

However, still on the subject of Christmas; as one delves into the ways of the Society, one realizes how they get round the matter, especially if there is a member of the family who is not a Witness. "You know, we shouldn't be eating these things—we are only doing it to please you!" The newer the convert, the greater eagerness to abolish Christmas, and it is these families which probably sit down to a meagre table, whilst brethren of greater experience partake of the usual delicacies on the quiet, with plenty of excuses!

Things are very difficult for Watchtower children, who have no Sunday School, nor any thing like Scouts or Guides or Brigades, not even a special Watchtower movement arranged for them. I had been a Christian Endeavourer before I joined them and naturally asked about anything like this. My word! I was of the devil to think of such things. *Let God be True* says "Moreover, there is no man-made organization that one can join when he becomes one of Jehovah's Witnesses". There is no Christmas, Palm Sunday, Easter, Whitsun or Harvest Thanksgiving and no Sunday observance, so how can anyone maintain Christian stability? As for Holy Communion, even children realize the sacredness of this but in the Watchtower Society it is observed only once a year. Even then the very few who wish to be part of the 144,000, the heavenly body of Christ, take Communion. Most Witnesses pass the bread and cup as a rejection of the Heavenly Kingdom, wishing rather to become part of the earthly body of the Kingdom. I only knew few who took the bread and wine. If you question a Watchtower child, he will repeat what he has been taught about all this. From a very young age they accompany older people on door-to-door work and recite the party pieces to order. Children love to do things like this, and repeat the Watchtower message as effectively as their seniors. When parents become Witnesses their children undergo a terrific psychological strain. Their homes, once happy and full of love, now have crumbling foundations. Men who have been holding good jobs get something much less important, bringing home lower wages and thus lowering the living standard to the poverty line. The fact that the women are forbidden to go out to work to stabilize the family finances makes things worse. Personally I found this state of poverty extremely depressing and hoped and prayed I would never be reduced to such a state of living. If only one member of the family becomes a Witness and enters the "truth", it means hell on earth for the others. The love for husband or wife has been replaced by love for the Organization, and the partner who was once loved in all the concerns of the home, is suddenly now spurned. The Witness is disgusted that he or she must tolerate living and sleeping with a "goat"! The grim aim follows, to destroy the other's personality in every way possible.

These very people, who are always talking about the persecution they suffer are in actual fact themselves the persecutors, and can and do pour boiling oil on the heads of the poor "goats". In some cases, however, the Witness leaves home—I imagine, much to the relief of the "goat" or "goats". Imagine how a child fares in such a case, especially when he is told that "God" is the cause of it all! If such children follow the believing parent they too must learn to live in opposition to the world. They are never taught any stories about Jesus, but, young as they are, are fed solely on adult publications. There is no incentive to do well at school, since the Witnesses hold that education is another of Satan's devices to conform people to his world. They just rub along unenthusiastically at school and then get any job they can, and then rub along in the same way; but their true life is in working for the Watchtower Society and ignoring the affairs of the day. Any development of creative gifts is foreign to the Society's purposes, and the life of its members is subordinated to its schemes.

I never met a Jehovah's Witness who on leaving school took a job calling for enthusiasm or initiative, or followed any vocation which brought some good to the world. They seem to prefer work, however menial, which allows full attention to be given to the purposes of the Society, so that their minds can continue to be engaged upon the Watchtower teachings. It is all a matter of mass existence, with no room for individuality.

In any Christian church you will often find that each member is a different personality from the others, and that each is employed upon something which he or she can do, each serving the Kingdom of God on earth, finding union with the others in worship, and giving God the glory for the vastness of His wonderful gifts to each of us.

In most denominations one finds a high percentage of nurses, but not with the Watchtower Society; for the words "vocation" or "healing" have no place with them. Yet what need there is in the world! Their blatant refusal to acknowledge this made me sick at heart; I used to lie in bed at night appreciating my home and all I had, but realizing that in the world around me there were sick or starving children, people still in refugee camps all these years after the war, cold and hungry, so that death would be a sweet mercy; old people dying in their rooms, not discovered for days or weeks. So I could go on, and the more I thought the more helpless I felt. The young people could have been guided to ask the Lord's divine will for their lives— certainly not to be content with dead-end jobs. What a waste of God-given brain and ability! What was life like for the child of Witness parents? They had so little—no Jesus who said "Suffer little children to come unto me; forbid them not!" The Watchtower Society was doing just that—forbidding the children access to His wonderful love. I could understand why Jehovah's Witnesses do not advocate bringing children into this world, for they have nothing to offer them, either spiritually or materially.

Do Jehovah Witness children fully realize the implications of what their parents lead them to believe, that our Heavenly Father is a God of destruction? Does a child really understand the import of this fearful doctrine of Armageddon?

It would be a wonderful thing for a Christian sometimes to have these little ones home to tea, and to show the child what love and understanding mean. It would be a real Christian witness, for Jesus said, "Whosoever shall receive this little child in my name receiveth me" (Luke 9:48).

You might very well be the first non-Jehovah's Witness person he or she had been in friendly touch with; normally they keep themselves very much to themselves.

25

A Closing Word

And if I be lifted up from the earth, will draw all men unto me. (John 12:32).

It is now nine years since I faced the facts squarely and realized with a shock that the Watchtower Society, the brethren of Jehovah's Witnesses, are a satanic force. I had been led to believe that this sect had the only way to God, so where was I to go? I have tried in these pages to depict my struggle until the light of the Lord Jesus Christ shone full on the falsities of the Watchtower doctrines, and these doctrines could not bear the light of His truth.

Many people suggest that Jehovah Witness zeal and enthusiasm could well be used to glorify Christ and the true Church, but that zeal and enthusiasm are inspired by the evil emotions of anger and hatred; hatred of the Church, which is the Body of Christ, and hatred of those who do not hold the Watchtower beliefs. This same hatred is poured also upon anyone in their homes who does not conform to their ideologies. During the last five years, thanks be to God, I have known His mercy, and my rebirth in His name is a witness to His redeeming power and His love for lost sheep. So far had I wandered that at the time of my conversion I didn't even own a Bible! I thank God for the unseen hand which saved me from any further deep involvement in this sect, just as William Schnell and Ted Dencher were so caught up in the web that only the grace of God released them. For William Schnell it was *Thirty Years a Watchtower Slave*; I had but ten years under their influence.

Since I started this book I have heard of more and more families splitting up through the intolerable arrogance of the Witnesses, and my heart is heavy, for this happened to me in my parents' home and in my own. I often wonder what they will answer to the Lord at the Judgement, when they are asked about the partner or the children He gave them, whom they have spurned and rejected in Jehovah's name. I had to learn humility, and not to look down on people of different denominations, for I sometimes found the old Watchtower arrogance would come into my heart. But a Church of England baptismal service which I attended taught me a lot. This was not long after I had been disillusioned by the Witnesses, and still I had much of this arrogance. I agreed to go to the baptism with a rather superior air; but that service might have been just for me. The Vicar said that there was no biblical authority for infant baptism, but he went on to speak of the terrible persecutions down the ages. In the early church people could not be publicly baptized in streams or rivers as Christ had commanded, for fear of their lives. They had to limit themselves to the sprinkling of water in secret places. They had their children baptized soon after birth, promising that they should be brought up in the Church, and at the same time they asked God-parents to look after the children, should their parents be imprisoned or killed—perhaps in the arena. You will notice that more than one God-parent was appointed— an indication of the perils of persecution. When I heard all this, I was ashamed of my arrogance. Would I have stood by my faith in those early days?

Because I have known and shared in such religious intolerance I am always grieved if I hear anyone quarrelling with people of another denomination, and seeming to claim all God's love and greatness for one of the churches. His Divine Spirit works in all the churches, and one only has to listen to people from every church to realize this. I thank the Lord for using members of all denominations to show me the love of Christ, and the way of the Cross which leads to Heaven.

We must adamantly refuse to argue about theology, but rather to base our talk upon mutual understanding, and keep the Lord Jesus Christ as the centre of every conversation. Thus we shall overcome the spirit of Satan and embrace instead the love of Christ. If we argue between ourselves, Christ is afflicted and hurt as He was by the leaders of religion who crucified Him nearly two thousand years ago.

Not so long ago I was in close contact with a member of a denomination far different from mine. Because we wanted to talk about Christ and His work we decided to talk about the things we held in common, and the blessing we received was remarkable. We started with Jesus, speaking of His way right through to His Second Coming, and this gave us much to talk about. "Where two or three are gathered together in my name there am I in the midst of them" (Matt. 18:20). One should not be surprised at this harmony, but rather praise the Lord that people of all denominations are looking forward to His Return.

> *He which testifieth these things saith,*
> *Surely I come quickly. Amen.*
> *Even so, come, Lord Jesus.*
> (Rev. 22:20)